THROUGH THE FIRE

One Woman's Experiences in
Surviving Domestic Violence

Written by
Harriet Cammock

This book is based on some true events, however, names, dates, and places are changed; all persons in this work are products of the author's imagination. Any resemblance to real persons, living or dead, is entirely coincidental.

All rights reserved. No part of this book may be reproduced by any form or by any electronic means, including information storage and retrieval systems, without written permission from the author, except by a reviewer who may quote brief passages, in a review.

If you purchased this book without a cover, you should be aware this book may be stolen property and reported as "unsold and destroyed". In such case, the author has not received any payment for this stripped book.

Copyright © Harriet Cammock, February 2011

Publisher Sadie Books, 215 E Camden Ave H11, Moorestown, NJ 08057 → 856-313-0548
sadie-books.com

ISBN-10: 098-1604730
ISBN-13: 978-0981604732
Library of Congress Control No. 2011920452

Book Layout / Cover Design
C Allen Design – callendesign.com

Other Published Books by Harriet Cammock
Visions
Musings of the Spirit

harrietcammock.org

Dedication

This book is dedicated to women who have suffered from domestic violence. To all the social workers, case workers, attorneys, police officers, other law enforcement agents, judges, prosecutors, who have watched over these cases, and worked tirelessly and sometimes stood by helplessly as the system failed to protect women from the hands of their abusive partners. On behalf of women who have been battered and beaten by their spouses, boyfriends, significant others; I dedicate this to you, this is your story. For women who haven't survived but whose children are reading this story, their memory lives on through the experiences written in this book, they are for whom this story is written. For the children who watched as Daddy beat Mommy and who had to live through the hellish experience that defined their lives, may you find healing in reading this. I am thankful to the counselors and ministers who listened to many women and encouraged them not to slit their wrists, and counseled them back to wholeness. To the women who help other women to plan escapes, who gave and donated their time, as well, and volunteered at shelters and other centers, this is your story. To you my dear reader, if you have been a victim of domestic violence, the fact that you are reading this means you have survived. And to you the reader who has never suffered, I am grateful you never suffered the harmful effects of domestic violence; this book is for you.

Acknowledgements

The Author wishes to thank the following persons: my daughter Alexandra, who stood beside me, who was my guiding light, my assistant Editor, and who was so brave and courageous, at times when she should have been a child, I thank her for her love and honesty. I am grateful she is now healed from the emotional scars of watching her mother endure domestic violence, and I wish for her all the love and successes this life has to offer. Words cannot tell how much I love you. I wish to thank my daughter, Anna Lisa, for her encouragement and love. I am so grateful you never had to live through this. I also wish to thank my mother, who was more than Mom, who stood by me through the years of abuse in my marriage, to my sisters, that they never live through this. I also wish to thank my friend and Editor, Janet Shan, who took time out of her busy schedule from writing The Hinterland Gazette to offer insight and support. Helen Silva, an attorney practicing in Orlando, Florida, who supported me through the divorce proceedings and many visits to court. A special thank you to my therapist, who was kind, professional and who guided me, supported me, and accompanied me to court and provided needed emotional support.

I also want to thank me, for not letting me down, for still believing in myself one day I would write this story,

Be blessed!

Preface

Through the Fire is my story of surviving domestic violence, and how I overcame the many struggles associated with it. This book is written to show the reader the scourge domestic violence is on our society. If you or anyone you know is experiencing domestic violence, contact the National Domestic Violence Hotline at thehotline.org

1

White Knight

People have often asked me exactly when the abuse began. But as I look back, it seems to have begun from the very beginning. It was November 22nd, 1989. It was unseasonably cool and dreary. And, it was my wedding day. The strangest things happened during that day. To my dismay, the photographer could not find his camera. He arrived at the wedding ready to take pictures, but he had no camera. Later on that day, I remember asking myself, *how can you be a photographer without carrying a camera?* Without a camera, there was no way to take pictures. Without pictures, there would be no tangible evidence of the wedding, no permanent record of that day. What saved us was a guest recorded the wedding on a camcorder. That recorded videotape has since been long lost. Apart from the marriage registration record, there is no other piece of evidence of the wedding ever taking place.

On that day, I had a frown on my face. I had been to many weddings before, and I had never seen a bride with a frown. But as I gazed in the mirror, my frowning face gazed right back at me. When I paused to really think about it, it seemed as though this wedding was the wrong thing to do.

My best friend, at the time, told me that if I were to actually marry this man, she would never come to my wedding, and, despite all of the years we spent as almost-sisters, I would never, ever see her again. She held true to this right up until the morning of my wedding; she called me and reminded of her promise. And despite my pleadings, she held fast to her pledge. I never saw her again. It was no small matter that my mother, bless her heart, told me I shouldn't marry him. When I asked her why, she said I just don't have a good feeling about him.

My father, who at the time, had spent most of his life absent from mine, also said don't marry him. My friends also said don't marry him. But nobody gave any concrete reasons why I shouldn't marry him. I remember one of his friends, who later became an acquaintance of mine, saying it was an unsuitable match.

But why on earth did no one tell me that he beat every woman whom he had ever been intimate with? Afterwards, I began to feel that maybe it's because domestic violence was not talked about in polite circles. People would not talk about a man hitting his wife because it just wasn't discussed. The woman was expected to deal with it and accept it. When my best friend made her statement, she hinted at a prior relationship, which Sam had, for which the woman involved had been violated; at the time it sounded like idle gossip. I thought I was in love and I felt that love would conquer all, and I would never know how things would work out. So I determined to give it a try.

Later on, I wondered *why did I get married? What on earth made me marry a man who, for all intents and purposes, seemed hell-bent on destroying my life?* As the old adage goes, love changes people, right? It might get better over time with love, right? But it never did. And so we got married. He arranged the honeymoon, and he took charge due to his desire to prove that he could handle anything. But the honeymoon never happened, as he forgot to reserve the hotel room. So, we never left and we never honeymooned. Looking back, it seemed as though his need for control was a precursor to the abuse, which began even before we were married.

We met while I was working. Sam walked into my office building asking for directions. I worked as an Administrative Assistant for a large company with regional offices in my hometown. As he walked into my office, he appeared to be very charming and *very* seductive. I couldn't resist him. He was tall, dark, and handsome. He had more worldly experience than I could ever dream of having. And he literally swept me off my feet. It seemed he was the answer to my dreams. Here comes the man, the white knight, riding in on his horse to my emotional rescue. Little did I know that hidden behind that charming, playful, and seductive exterior was a mad man intent on ravaging my life. I had no idea about the dangers hidden in the complexities of his personality, and I was incapable of grasping what made him the monster he later revealed himself to be. All I knew, at the time, was that everything I had been looking for was wrapped up in this man.

As women, we've all grown up hearing stories of marriages. The stories we're told as girls paint marriage out to be a fairy tale - a fairy tale that will never be replicated in real life. I grew up thinking that one day I was going to marry someone who would make me forget all those things I wanted to forget, all the struggles and trials that had plagued me since childhood. But what they didn't tell me was that I was to be careful about what I wished for. But I was not thinking about that when Sam walked into my office, representing everything that I had hoped and dreamed for in a man. And I *thought* I was ready for it.

When Sam initially asked me out, I politely declined, playing the 'wait and see' game. But, I eventually wore down under his relentless pressure to become a part of his life and to go out with him. I should have known something was wrong when he insisted that our first date be at his house. But at the time, I just thought he wanted to impress me with how much he had acquired. So we went out to his house and hung out, then I left and went home. He was accommodating to a fault; he made it seem as though he'd been waiting for me all his life.

When I told some friends about him, they weren't surprised that I had been so easily duped by his charms. My friends had heard of him and apparently, he had a 'history' with women They didn't tell me all of it, but I assumed that it meant he had been a ladies' man, and was used to getting his way with women. Some of them made it clear that it was not a good idea for me to be with him, but I somehow made up in my mind that everything would be all right and that it would work out. I didn't give their suggestions any thought. Some felt that he was too experienced for me and too matured for me.

Others felt he was too controlling and would not allow me to develop into whom I was created to be. In hindsight, it is now clear that they knew what they were talking about. Sam engaged in a deliberate program of eliminating my life as if I never existed before I met him. Control is too kind a word to describe the games he played with my life to ensure in every aspect he was in control.

Before long, I moved in with him. The first few weeks went by without incident. Within six months, however, the mask of charm and cool fell off. He began a program of exacting as much control over me as possible. Suddenly my friends weren't good enough for me to hang around. I couldn't call anyone and no one could call me. He screened my phone calls and he determined whether I would speak to anyone or not. Not even my closest family members could call and hold a conversation with me. Little by little, he engaged in a program of alienation and isolation, removing me from the presence of my friends and replacing his friends as mine.

And yet, I still didn't see anything wrong with that. It seemed to me that he just excessively cared about me. I couldn't see through the disguise that he used to mask his true intentions. Later, as the masks fell off, I would see him for what he really was. But by then, it would have been too late. So here we are, on the wedding day, ready to take the plunge into long-term commitment. No photographers to record the day. Just the living memory of the nightmare my life would become.

Within the first two or three months, life proceeded normally. There were no issues, no quarrels; it was as if someone told him to remain calm for the first few months. Sam had this Dr. Jekyll/Mr. Hyde kind of personality. He could be anything you wanted him to be. He could be kind, he could be less controlling, outgoing. But most of the time, he was a prison warden (to me only). He would let me out when he felt that I'd had too much confinement; he would keep me in if he felt I'd had too much exposure, etc. And sometimes, his rage would flare up at random intervals; think 'hair trigger temper', if you can. And when his fury was unleashed, it burned everyone in its path to a scalding point. I remember thinking that I lived in a gilded cage, sort of like a padded cell. I could look out at the world, but I couldn't get out. He used to say, "why do you want to go out, everything you need is here", as if he was all I needed. When I now think back on it, it is unbelievable that I could have fallen under his spell and was convinced by his façade.

In the early years of our marriage, he would always leave town and take overseas trips. By leaving town, he was concealing the violent parts of his personality from me. He didn't want me to know just how violent all of his personalities could become. As our marriage progressed, I was exposed to more and more of *his* friends who were inclined to keep the secrets of Sam's past hidden from me.

Maybe I should have paid more attention to the 'suggestions' my friends made earlier. I should have taken heed too, because stories of his pattern of abusing women were emerging and appeared to be more fact than fiction. My best friend had been right. Sam never liked her from the beginning because he knew if our friendship continued, she would become a greater influence on me than he wanted.

After we got married, it became normal for him to spend six months away from home, working overseas. During these absences, life would go as normal as I was free to work and socialize the way I wanted. I joined community groups and went out with my friends, as any normal person would do. It was usually on his return trips, that his violent 'urges' rose up, and whenever this happened he would concoct an excuse to leave town.

Whenever he was home, I had to tread carefully around him because being around him was like walking on eggshells. On the other hand, there was his nice-guy side. He was very sociable; he was considered to be the life of the party, and he was extremely charming to all women he encountered as well as being an extremely persuasive man. Anything he wanted to have was just a matter of being able to talk his way into it.

Sam had a wide group of friends. And did he ever have the most loyal, faithful and trusting friends; his personality inspired great devotion from his comrades. It was sociopathic, his behavior; he became anything you wanted him to become. So whenever he came back from his long trips, he was *Mr. All Around Nice Guy*. He had stories to tell, parties to throw, parties to attend, etc. And, he was always one for throwing parties at our house. So when I started to tell people about the abuse, not one soul believed me. To everyone else, Sam was everyman, the charming and nice, worldly everyman. Only to me was he a monster.

2
Sergeant

Here is where the waters began to turn to mud. After a while, Sam's controlling inclination escalated. The first time was when he returned from one of his trips in December of 1990. He decided that we should celebrate New Year's Eve at *his* friend's house. I wanted to celebrate it with some of my friends at a party they were hosting. Of course, that was completely out of the question. It seemed as though he convinced *his friends* to have a party just so I would have to go to that party instead of being in the company of *my friends*. This avenue presented him with further control over me.

My cousin came over to our house, as we were getting ready to go. I had told her to come because I had suspected Sam might be violent towards me. I thought her presence would act as a buffer. Sam had bought me a dress that he thought was suitable enough for me to wear. I had originally bought my own dress, but he felt I should wear the dress *he* bought me. He claimed that because he bought the dress at an expensive store and he'd spent a lot of money on it, I should be thankful for it. I didn't like the dress because it made me look matronly and old.

But Sam insisted that I wear the dress. Because I wanted to wear a more demure dress that didn't look so formal, we had a very sharp exchange of words. He suddenly grabbed me by my throat, wrapping his long, claw-like fingers around my throat, and he slapped me directly across my face. Then he pushed me against the dresser, in the bedroom, causing intense pain to reverberate through my small body in waves. After a moment, I gathered my bearings and managed to articulate. "Don't you *touch* me like that again," I said bravely but precariously. "You're my wife. I can do anything I want to you," he snapped in his gravelly voice.

Within seconds, my cousin flew into the bedroom and shouted, " Sam, What are you doing! Take your hands off her, are you crazy!" And he dropped his hands to his side, as though he were the victim, and calmly walked out of the room. I was shaking like a leaf. I sat down on the edge of my bed and said to my cousin, "This is exactly what I was afraid of."

As I sat there, I *still* would not listen to the tranquil, small voice in the back of my head, telling me that something was glaringly wrong with this picture. I just thought that these things were normal and married people have disagreements like this all the time. I couldn't see the big picture. The big picture was that because I *resisted* his control, he was going to prove to me that he would do whatever it took for me to *submit* to his control.

In the end, I gave in and we went to the party that *he* selected because Sam made it very clear if his orders were not strictly followed, I would have no peace. Without a doubt, I was miserable. I absolutely hated being at that awful party, but I said to myself, *it's only one night. And besides, there's always next year.* Within a few days, Sam was gone again on one of his excursions out of the country. He was gone from around March to September of that year, all of six months. It was his pattern to return home as soon as the weather became cooler, right around Labor Day. The next time he returned home, I had no clue I was about to see more of his true colors.

On his return home, the first announcement Sam made was, "Some things are going to have to change around here." I said, "Like what?"

"Some of the things you've been doing are unacceptable, and going to *have* to be corrected."

"*What* things?" I snapped.

"First of all, you're not going to go out as often as you do." In order for you to understand why this pronouncement made no sense, you first have to know that I wasn't one to go out very often. I was one of those people who believed that one's social patterns should change once married.

"What do you mean by 'going out'? I don't go out."

"Well, some of the people who you talk to."

"Like *what* people I talk to?" I was getting impatient now.

Sam continued, "Well, you're going to have to change your friends. You're married now, so your friends have to be more like my friends. You can't do some of the things you've been doing."

"Goodness, like *what* things? I asked.

He just kept on "Like that girl you go to who does your hair."

"That *girl*? She's a *woman*, you know. And she's married and she has her own life."

"Well, you have to change that and some other stuff, too…"

On and on he went about my imperfect friends, my imperfect schedule, and my all-around imperfect life. I got the feeling that the only reason it was imperfect was because none of what I did suited what he *thought* I should be doing. *Who is he to tell me I should switch around my entire life just so it can line up with his? And then, he has the nerve to do it under the 'you're married now' guise.*

At the time, I was working. And *my* income was the one that provided the stability, health insurance, house bill payments, food, and car, all while he either sat at home or was traveling abroad. For the life of me, I couldn't understand why he thought he should exact that much control over my life, when my livelihood was financing his endeavors. He supported his threats to 'make some changes' by making sure that every waking second of my life was a living hell when I didn't follow his orders; he nagged, hassled, complained, grumbled, shoved me around, etc. After a while, it became more expedient to just do what he said as opposed to asserting my freedom.

When I left for work in the mornings, he was the first person to call my office. Why? Just so he could make sure I was actually where I said I would be at the time. Then, he would call me at lunchtime to ensure that I didn't leave the office unnecessarily. Then, he would call again between three and five. And you know he called just before it was time for me to leave the office. To add insult to injury, he would *time* me from when I left work to when I got home. If I wasn't home at exactly the same time every day, or, God forbid, I did not answer the office phone, I received no end of misery about it. He was like the drill sergeant of my worst nightmares.

It all began to finally dawn on my young and naïve mind that there *must* be something wrong with this picture. But I didn't have any frame of reference because outside of the girls I worked with (who were all unmarried), the only married friends I had were *his* friends. And because they were *his* friends, they weren't going to enlighten me on whether or not this behavior was normal.

I finally broke down and admitted to my mother all that was going on. In her wisdom, she said that she couldn't remind me that she *did* tell me to never marry him because it makes no sense in crying over spilled milk. She just kept repeating that it's okay and this shall pass. It never did pass.

As time went on, he tightened his controlling mechanisms. It was as if a noose were constricting around my neck. Simple things that any woman should be allowed to do were strictly forbidden in that house. When I left work, I had to come directly home; there was no getting my hair done, no shopping, and no socializing with my friends. Everywhere I would go, Sam had to be there. If I wanted to go somewhere and he could not go with me, then I simply wasn't allowed there at all. Even during the few times I was allowed to go out, I couldn't drive myself; *he* had to be the one to drop me off, and *he* had to be the one to pick me up. Anywhere he didn't want to go was somewhere I was not allowed to go, *period*.

Later on that year, I became pregnant with our daughter. She was born three years after we were married. With her birth, I experienced something ten times as strong as joy. At the moment she was born, I realized that somehow, some way, my life had to change. I could not continue to live in an environment where I was subjected to any level of emotional abuse and control, especially with a child now in the picture. It became apparent it was emotionally unhealthy to raise a child with that level of expectation. What kind of life would she have if every day, she grew up seeing her mother be ill treated, and abused by her father?

As time passed and I tried to work my way through the nightmare my life had become, we relocated to Florida. That was when the *worst* of the worst began. Those last three years of our marriage were the defining moments. Those were the years when abuse escalated to unprecedented levels. Sam now fit the profile of an abuser and he began a quest to make my life a living hell. For me, it was the beginning of the end.

We lived in a small town named Deltona, north of Orlando, in Florida. We moved to Deltona because a friend suggested we buy a house there because housing prices were so low. Our house was in a subdivision that was bordered by woods. There were days when I felt as though I was literally living in a jungle. But, the difference was the jungle outside was *nothing* compared to the jungle in our home.

By this time we had been together for over ten years. It was easy to say that our marriage had seen its fair share of ups and downs. Nonetheless, life continued. At the time, the way I saw it was I was trying to make the best out of a bad situation. Our daughter was now five years old, and she was enrolled in the local elementary school. That alone presented a whole new host of problems, as Sam was not the kind of parent who believed in letting our daughter socialize outside of school; and he also wasn't the PTA-joining parent either. Of course, those were my attributes, but like I said: he was the drill sergeant. And in our home, anything he said was law. And anybody who didn't follow suit paid a *very* dear price.

3
Over

I knew my marriage was over around late 1997 or early 1998. When we bought that house in the small town and moved in, I remember gazing at the forest just outside the kitchen window, wondering *what had I done*. The rush of unpacking, enrolling our daughter in school, looking for jobs and buying new furniture provided enough of a distraction to keep a strained neutrality in the house. But the one obvious lacking ingredient was peace. At least, peace for me.

Abuse has many faces and can take many forms. One of the forms of abuse popular with Sam was financial abuse. Although we had a joint account, *he* dictated how much went in, and how much came out. If I went to the store, I was only allowed to spend $50. If I spent $50 and one cent, I was slapped, like a child getting disciplined for being disobedient.

I knew the end of our marriage was coming because I insisted on going to church as often as I could. For me, going to church was the only social interaction I had with anyone outside of his friends. But of course, he made this task especially difficult. Like a child, I had to ask for his explicit permission to go. And of course, he would sometimes relent and grant me permission, but most of the time his answer was a solid *no*. Just like he used to time me on my way from work to home, he timed me on my way from church to home. But I pushed through all of that because church provided me with a mental escape from the turmoil I was enduring at home. Church was my euphoric paradise, the complete opposite of the icy hell I endured on a daily basis.

When his usual controlling tactics were not giving him as much control as he thought he should have, Sam would up the ante.

This day started out just like any other day. I knew I was going to be beaten; I could see it just by looking in his cruel face. It was his custom to wake up before I did (usually around five in the morning) just to watch me sleep. In those days, because of the tension in the household, I rarely received a good night's sleep. Many nights as I lay down, I would be in anticipation of a confrontation. My mind was in turmoil as I was always watchful, always on alert, always expecting *something* to happen. It got to the point where I just started anticipating his fists; it seemed anything would provoke him. I spent countless nights, praying, believing, *and hoping* that he would not come near me. I spent many of my waking hours praying that today is the day I will not be beaten within an inch of my life.

This particular morning, I knew he had it in for me because as soon as my eyes struggled open, they met with his red eyes, staring back at me with fury. His hands were folded across his chest, as he sat there just *staring* at me. "I've been waiting for you to get up," Sam said in a measured tone. At that time, I wished so strongly that I could close my eyes again and pretend this day had passed, and that I was living some time very far into the future. I wished that I wouldn't have to endure what was surely coming my way in the next few moments. I silently prayed *oh God, make it be quick this time*.

I had no choice but to slowly sit up so I could start my day. Our daughter, Alexandra, was sleeping in her room, which was strange enough in itself because she usually always slept in our room in a chair that I would sit in to watch TV. I guess she felt that she had to protect Mommy from Daddy. But last night, I convinced her that it wouldn't be so bad for her to sleep in her own room. During the preceding days, he had been so nice and calm. I took advantage of this and persuaded her to sleep by herself because I wanted her to experience a normal life as much as she could. I wanted her to feel just like any other normal child, by going to *her* bed at nights and sleeping in *her* very own room.

As I sat up, Sam turned to me saying, "Where do you think you're going?" My heart thudded so hard against my chest that I thought it would surely pop out of my body. That my heart was beating was a miracle because I was so afraid that I could barely open my mouth to speak, much less to breathe and give oxygen to my brain. I didn't know what he was going to do. All I did was hope that he would just let me get off the bed. I had the sudden urge to pee and I couldn't get past him to the bathroom. Somehow, he must have known how much I needed to pee, and he intended to keep me from using the bathroom.

So he used his body and his threatening presence to keep me imprisoned on the bed. He knew that I was fearful. By his reasoning, if he kept me this way, he would keep me imprisoned on the bed. Much to my humiliation and much to his pleasure, I would eventually have to beg him to keep from peeing on myself.

I looked at him and I said, "I'm going to start getting Alex ready for school." He said, "You're not leaving this house."

"It's only school. It's not far; only five minutes away. I'll be right back…I *promise* I'll be right back…" I responded.

He retorted, "*I said* you are not leaving this house."

If I didn't give him advanced notice about anything I wanted to do, he saw it as a surprise attack and an offence against him; he would punish me accordingly. So we had discussed the night before that I would take Alex to school.

"Ok," I said, trying to placate him. "Well, will you take her?"

"You don't tell me what to do!" he yelled.

"Alright. Well, somehow, she must get to school."

"What do you mean by *somehow*? Do you have somebody else on the side that'll be taking her to school? If I don't drive you and if I don't drive her, how is she going to get to school?" His voice had taken on an unrecognizable pitch, a very angry, very infuriated pitch.

"Ok, then we'll work this out some other way." I just wanted to get out of that bedroom and I was willing to say whatever he wanted to hear to do so.

"How are we going to work it out? Are you telling me what do? Didn't I tell you that you don't tell me what to do? Who *told* you that you could tell *me* what to do? I'M THE ONE WHO TELLS YOU WHAT TO DO!"

He lashed out with an open-palmed slap across my face, but I ducked. I wasn't fast enough to out-maneuver him, and there ensued what I would call The Chase. I rolled away from him and jumped over to the other side of the bed, crawled on my knees trying to get to the door to get out of the room, but he was entirely too quick. He made it to the door before I did and slammed it shut. Now, I was in the room alone with him, with no way out.

I knew what was coming next, and it was his foot hitting me square in my side.

I just sat there and begged, "Please...let's just get her to school. I'm begging you please..." I just sat there as he stood over me and looked as though he were contemplating what to do to me. To my relief, he growled, "You're lucky. You get away *this* time."

The next thing I heard were my daughter's footsteps running to the door and her angelic little voice saying, "Mommy, are you alright?" She opened the door, just as he opened the door. She bravely pushed past him and looked up dead in his eyes and asked "Daddy, did you hit Mommy?" He said, "No sweetheart, I didn't touch your Mommy. Your Mommy is a bad lady and even though she deserves to be hit, Daddy didn't hit her. Daddy is a nice guy. Come here and let me tell you how much Daddy loves you."

I sat on the floor recoiling in horror at what this man had done. The emotional ramifications of what he had just done to me and to our daughter dawned on me in the most horrific of ways. That Dr. Jekyll/Mr. Hyde character had just come into play; the man who was about to beat the living daylights out of me is the same man who was now consoling my child and telling her that I deserved to be beaten senseless. As I sat on the floor contemplating this, a small, still voice in my head told me that *this too shall pass*. This will come to an end some day. The question was, *how?*

I eventually got her dressed and prepared for school. Just before she was supposed to leave, he went to start the car in the garage. She pulled me into her room and said, "Mommy, all day long, I want you to stay in my room. If you stay in my room, he will not come in here and touch you. So don't say *anything* to him. Just stay in my room until I come home from school, ok Mommy?"

I couldn't believe my 5-year-old daughter was going to be my defender. I could not believe that he had emotionally damaged her to the point where she felt she had to defend her Mommy from her Daddy. At that time, I was as skinny as they come. I was 5'1 and I weighed 120 pounds, soaking wet. He was 6'2 and he was 230 pounds of muscle, brawn and anger. And to think that a 5-

year old child was going to be the defense between he and I was unfathomable.

She gave me one last tight hug, and as I watched her walk away from me, I knew that when he returned from dropping her off, I might as well just prepare myself for the armada he was probably going to unleash against me. As she got in the car, I heard her tell him, "Daddy, if you touch my Mommy before I come back from school, I am going to scream so loudly, the neighbors will hear and call the police. Do you hear me?" And all he could say was "Yes, dear, I hear you." And she got in the car and they drove off to school.

I sat down and all I could do was cry. I started thinking *what kind of life have I subjected this child to? How do I get her, and myself, out of this? Where do I start planning?* I had no money to my name. I couldn't work in the United States because I was not yet authorized to do so. As an immigrant, when you come to the United States, you have to apply for and receive a Work Authorization. You take that document down to the Social Security office and apply for a social security number. This you have to present to any prospective employer before you can be hired. I had entered the country on a visitor's visa; in order to work someone has to sponsor you. In my case my husband was the sponsor, but what do you know, he was going to use the process to further keep me trapped in this hell of a marriage and use this to his advantage as much as possible. Without a work permit, you cannot work and if you do not work, how do you save money to plan a getaway?

The thing is I often contemplated going back home, but knowing Sam, I knew he would never give me a chance to leave with Alex. He would do everything in his power to prevent me from leaving. I knew I couldn't leave without her, as I was fairly sure I would never see her again. I didn't know anyone who could take me to the airport. How could I leave? Even if I asked my Mom to buy the tickets, Sam made sure I didn't drive; he takes Alex to school, and he kept the keys to the car. Sometimes, he would even unplug the telephone from the wall and take it with him in the car. I used to pray there would never be a fire at home because I wouldn't have been able to call the fire department or call the emergency services. No wonder I felt trapped because escape didn't seem possible.

Sam did not work so he was always in the house, and when he left, he took the keys to the car with him. How was I going to get out of this?

4
Escape

I picked up a pen and paper and began to write. I wrote how I felt, about how it began, and about my observations. Slowly, but surely, writing became therapeutic. Writing became my coping mechanism. It made the abuse *almost* bearable. I had to develop a means of escape because I couldn't physically escape. But I could escape mentally. So I would imagine what my future life would be like. I would imagine that my daughter and I would one day live free from this horror and that one-day it would all be just an experience that was far behind us. We would be free to do the normal things that mothers and daughters do.

Another means of escape for me was watching TV, and watching a lot of it. And even then, I had to be careful what I watched; but for *him*, certain shows or movies were a problem. I couldn't let him know about my main source of escape, which was writing. If he ever found out about my writing, not only would I pay the severe consequences, but also, he would destroy my writing thereby destroying my daily escape to freedom. So I hid all the journals, I wrote, under the bed in the guest room.

In fact, the guest room became my refuge. I used to run in there and shut the door when it all became too much. For some reason, he would never come in there to bother me. I started planning how I could escape. I had no control over money. I could never get more than enough money to buy groceries, so that allotment was already very little. Nonetheless, I started to plan.

My nearest relatives lived 1,500 miles away in Detroit. The question that plagued me for some time was how do I get to them with my daughter? I had no friends because, as usual, my friends were his friends. I had no income, no savings. So what was I to do?

I knew that he probably suffered from schizophrenia because for two or three weeks, life in the house would be normal without a blip or disturbance on the radar. Literally, nothing would happen. And then suddenly, out of the blue, would come a wrath-filled outburst.

The next time one of these outbursts would come was just another normal day. In fact, it was quite bright and sunny outside, but there were no sunny feelings inside our home. I could feel that something was wrong. The previous night, despite the fact that Alex had slept in the chair next to my bed, I had an unexplained fitful sleep. I woke up the next day knowing that deep down, something was wrong. Everything appeared to be normal. He knew how to pretend that he was going to be all right and calm. I didn't realize anything was afoot until after he had dropped Alex off at school.

After the last almost incident, he hadn't laid a hand on me or even so much as come near me. After he would drop our daughter off at school, he would normally go buy his daily lottery ticket, and then go buy his paper, and usually he wasn't back home for a few hours. After a while, he developed a pattern of being gone for hours at a time after dropping our daughter off at school.

But this morning, I could feel that today would be the day I would be in physical pain. I had barely had time to wash the dishes in the sink before I heard the garage door rolling up, signaling his return. *That's odd*, I thought, *he's normally not back for a while*. I felt something heavy and cold drop in the pit of my stomach. My nerves skyrocketed when he opened the garage door.

I couldn't believe the expression he had on his face. He changed completely. Yesterday, he was smiling and happy as a lark. Today, he looked like a bat straight out of hell.

"What are you doing?" he asked sharply.

"I'm cleaning up."

"You never wash the dishes clean enough." I didn't say anything because by this point, I had learned it was best to keep my mouth shut. Ironically, we had a dishwasher, and whenever I was done rinsing the dishes in the sink, I'd put them in the dishwasher and turn it on to finish the job. So if the dishwasher was washing the dishes, how was I not cleaning them enough? But I kept my mouth shut for the sake of my safety.

"I'm tired of the way things are around here. They have to change. You have too much control of that child. You tell her what to do. She listens to you too much. You're always telling her what to do and you set her up against me."

Stupefied, I said, "How do I do that?"

"She's always telling me not to touch you! Who is telling her those things? Who told her that I touched you? How am I touching you? What am I doing to you? Why are you telling her lies? Why are you telling her to tell me not to touch you?"

"But," was all I could stammer out before he snapped again.

"Don't answer me! Don't talk back to me!"

He was standing at the garage door that led into the kitchen, and I was still standing at the sink. Then he started to walk towards me. I instinctively started backing into the refrigerator, trying to get away from him. It was like facing down a wild animal. If you show the animal that you're afraid, it attacks you even more viciously than it normally would. *'I can't show him how afraid I am'* was all I could think. But as I backed up, I placed my hand on the counter where I kept the steak knives.

"What are you doing?" he accused, his voice taking on new characteristics.

"Nothing."

"Are you threatening me?"

"No, I'm not. I would never do that…"

"Well, I'm just letting you know I don't like the way you treat that child, and I don't like how you bring that child up against me. I don't like it. And you'd better stop if you know what's good for you."

And, just like the whole thing never happened, he walked past me, and went and sat down to watch TV.

I went back to the sink to continue washing the dishes. I exhaled slightly and thought *it's over*. But it wasn't.

As I continued tidying up the house and wishing that I could work, the phone rang. It was a close friend of mine. She had the most exciting news I could have ever dreamt of hearing.

"Girl, I have a little get-together planned," she gushed through the receiver. "But I know how *he* is, so let me talk to him first so that the trouble doesn't fall on your head."

I handed him the phone and told him who it was.

"So? What does she want?" he snarled.

"I don't know. I think she just wants to say hi. Just talk to her for me, please?"

He took the phone, transformed his voice into the charming Mr. Nice Guy, and spoke casually with her. She explained to him what plans she had, and his interest piqued. Of course, being the control-freak that he was, he had to ask what kind of dinner it was, who would be there, what would the women do, while the men socialized, how many persons, etc.

Now imagine this scene folding out before me. I'm a grown woman, and an intelligent grown woman at that. I didn't have a college degree, but I had some college education (*far* more than he did) and I also had been very successful in the hotel industry. Despite all of this, I had to sit there and listen to a man determine whether I would go out to a friend's house or not.

I thought to myself *let me just play the part this one time because it will bring me one step closer to being able to raise my daughter in freedom.* She worked it out with him, and after they were through speaking, he hung up the phone. He never passed the phone back to me or even asked if I wanted to continue speaking to her. I had no say in that matter.

Then, he turned to me and said, "This is my country. *I* am in charge here, not you. *I* am the citizen here, not you. You have to do what *I* say. You can't do anything or go anywhere because *I* have rights, and you don't."

He made sure I understood that he was the citizen, so he knew the system better than I did. And even though he and I were legally married and I could have easily obtained my green card just by being married to him, he never allowed this to even happen. It's as if he wasn't just playing a power game in his mind, but he was playing a power game with the system as well. Until I was processed (the only way that would happen is through him because he was the citizen and also my husband), there was nothing I could do.

And you already know that he made a big deal of it. In our native country, due to my thriving employment, I'd had many influential friends. So Sam felt the wheels had turned in his favor, giving him control over my life thereby causing me to become a train wreck, if he wanted me to be. Here I was in this land, cut off from my friends and influence, disenfranchised and dispossessed fearing that if I left, I would never see my child again. He wielded the ultimate power trip as he felt he had me completely under his control. And he *knew* that and he used it to his advantage.

When my friend, Sally, said she was planning a dinner, what she was really trying to do was get me away from him. The only way she could do that was to make him a part of the gathering, so that while the men talked sports, the women could get together and plan. She was going to help me plan how I could get away while I was there. This was the only route she could take to accomplish this task.

After he got through speaking to my friend on the phone, aside from his little 'reminder' to me, he didn't speak for a very long time; he just went on watching TV. And then he fell asleep. I've always wondered how abusive men were able to fall asleep or go into relaxation mode before the TV immediately after beating you senseless.

I thought this would be the opportune time to escape! I thought. I could go and pick up Alex from school and we could run away to somewhere far and safe. But then I didn't have a debit card, so there was no way to get any money from the bank. And even if I took the car, where would Alex and I sleep tonight? On the *roadside?* My nearest family members were almost 2,000 miles away. How would I get to them? What could I do?

I sat there and worked it out in my head from his perspective. If I did leave with my daughter, he would probably call the police and declare me a missing person. And knowing him, he would tell them that I stole the car, kidnapped his daughter, and am trying to take her out of the country where he would never see her again. I didn't have my papers, which means I didn't have rights. Because I didn't have rights, they would lock me up, then send me back home, and I would never see my daughter again. I couldn't do anything at all.

He knew that I didn't have any rights and he knew that was something that made me scared because I was afraid of being locked up. And he would probably even go as far as lying and saying that I am an unfit parent. This man was capable of doing anything he wanted to achieve his goal of destroying me. So I sat down, picked up my journal and thought, *somehow, I'm going to get out of this.*

A few days later, Sally came over to pick me up and invited both of us to her house to have dinner. While we were at her house, she took me into her bathroom while her husband and Sam were talking. "Now, we've *got to have a plan.* Here's what we need to do. We need to get you out of that house, away from here, and to your mother in Detroit. That's what we need to do."

"But he's going to come and take Alex away because he knows that I don't have any legal rights here and he would probably take me to court. And because he's the citizen, the courts would grant him custody and I would never see her again!" I was frantic with the very thought of never being able to never hold my sweet child in my arms again.

"Foolishness! Sally said "This happens to people all the time and they get out of it with their children intact!"

"No it doesn't! Think realistically with me. If he goes to court, he is going to end up with custody and I will *never see my child again!* It's ok for me to go back home because I was always somebody there, but how am I going to go back without my child?"

"Well, I guess you're right," she conceded. "But what are you going to do in the mean time? You *have* to get out of there!"

"I don't know yet! But I have to find a way to run away with her. I can't just leave her because if I leave her with him, he's going to destroy her as much as he's destroying me now! She deserves to have a life filled with peace and love and that's a life I can give her, something that he can't! I don't know what I'm going to do yet, but I'll figure it out."

"Ok," she said, finally seeing the truth in my reasoning. "How much longer before your papers situation is finished?"

"I don't know. The lawyer says that in a few months I am to file for my work permit and my social security card."

"Good, when you get that done, we're going to get you a job and start the plan."

"Ok." I believed that my situation would actually change as quickly as I imagined it would.

5
No Way Out

For a while after that, he was so nice. For the next three months, leading up to the New York visit to the lawyer, nothing happened. We went to the lawyer and obtained the work permit and the social security card.

I've always thought with all that I'd been dealt in life, it would only be fair to have this kind of story happen to someone else, as obnoxious as this sounds. I would have obviously preferred to be the bystander as opposed to being the innocent victim. But that's not the way it happened. This was *my* story that *I* would have to live with for the rest of my life. But the story's not over yet, because I was still living it every day.

I was still breathing and living in this dark nightmare that my life had become. There seemed to be no way out of it. I felt that having a work permit and a social security card meant that I would have some sort of mobility and freedom. But that was not the intention of the man to whom I was married.

Sam had no intention of enabling me to be free enough to leave him. His greatest fear was that I would leave and that would render him without control. When a woman works, she's empowered. And an empowered woman is a dangerous woman. She now has the power to think and move freely. *That* was not part of his plan at all.

On our return from New York, the first thing I sat down to do was to get a job. My friend, Sally was true to her promise. My first job was as a babysitter. I babysat an elderly lady, who in the declining years of her life, was struggling to maintain her sanity. It really was the easiest thing I had ever done because all I had to do was sit in a room with her while the registered nurse came and attended to her daily needs. My job was to sit there to call 911 or a relative in case she began to deteriorate too quickly for the nurse to arrive. It was good and easy money. The only problem was separation from Alex. I would sometimes be gone for two or three days at a time.

Even though I missed her, Sam did everything in his power to make sure she was well cared for in my absence. He wanted to have the money I earned so he could chock it away over time and so I would never have access to it. The average person might be asking, *how could you work and not have the very money you earned?* Well, even though we had a joint account, I opened an account in my own name. What I neglected to do was get a post office box where the bank statements for this account would go to; instead, the bank statements went to our house.

You don't have to take a guess at who always ran to the mailbox before I did. As a matter of fact, he would wait on the mailman every day, without pause. And once he got the mail, he would open *all* of it, including mine. This is how he found out about my bank account. I paid *dearly* for that.

I came home one evening. He was strangely quiet. I had previously noticed how quiet Alex had been when he came to pick me up from work. She sat in the back of the car, very subdued. I even asked her what was wrong; she couldn't answer. Apparently, he found out about the secret bank account and had been quarreling and grumbling about it all day. She knew this, but there was no way for her to communicate the terror that awaited me when I would get home.

He was too slick to hit me in the car while we were driving. There were too many cars driving up and down the street. Sam was careful not to leave witnesses to his evil acts. He and I were the witnesses. Sam thought no one would believe me. In fact, one of his threats, which he carried out frequently, was, as he put it, 'to hit me in soft places'. Alex, the other unintended victim, was whom he thought he could win over by telling her and showing her that her mother deserved to be treated this way. He wanted to convince her

Mommy was a bad person whom Daddy had to discipline because Mommy didn't do what Daddy wanted her to do. Sam was sure that Alex would love him and side with him against Mommy.

I used to wonder what child do you know of would side with a cruel man against her mother? I thought he was quite delusional, but I knew I had to keep my thoughts to myself. I feared that one-day, he would turn on Alex.

He waited until we got inside the house that served as the headquarters for the nightmare of my existence. As soon as we walked in from the garage door to the laundry room, he grabbed me by my throat.

"HOW DARE YOU!" he shouted.

"How dare I what?" I choked out between the gasps.

"Daddy leave mommy alone!" came the desperate cries of Alex.

I tried to grab onto the washing machine for support. I tried to say something, but he yanked me into the kitchen by the collar of my turtleneck sweater. He grabbed the bank statement that had come in the mail, off the counter.

"How could you do this? Who *told* you that you could do this?" He threw me against the kitchen wall.

"Didn't I *tell* you that you couldn't do this? Didn't I *tell* you this was forbidden?" He seemed to be getting angrier at each word.

At this point, I was backing into the back of the couch in the family room (the kitchen and family rooms were adjacent to each other). He matched my every step. I was ducking to avoid his blows. He was so filled with fury that his eyes looked like they were sprouting bouts of fire at me.

As I got closer to the couch, I knew, then, I was in for it. I felt a hard slap across my face. I blinked as I tried to focus on the stars I saw swimming before my vision cleared. To this present day, I remember the effects of that blow. Unsuccessfully, I tried to blink the stars away. He pulled my hair and used it to drag me across the floor into the bedroom. By this time, my daughter was beside herself, hysterically screaming for Daddy to leave Mommy alone. It wasn't enough.

Once he got to the bedroom door, he tried to slam it shut so he could have his way with me, but I clung to the door and tried to use my feet to kick him away. But his viciously powerful legs wouldn't give under the force of my small feet. It was then that he began to beat me mercilessly with his fists. When he was done, I had remarkably survived. But I was black and blue everywhere my eyes could see.

My daughter had managed to run into the room and she tried to use the phone to dial 911. She was unaware *he* had unplugged all the telephones from their sockets in the wall, leaving us with no way to contact outside help.

Now, for the first time, I realized that I was trapped inside a loveless and violent marriage that was on a path to destroy my life.

As I sat there on the floor, I crawled into the walk-in closet looking for peace and comfort. And I sat in there and refused to come out. I closed the door, and my daughter came in shortly after I did.

"Mommy, I'm staying with you."

"No," I protested through a busted lip, "I want you to leave. It's too dark in here for you honey."

"No, Mommy, we can turn the light on," she protested.

"It's entirely too dark for you to be in here…I'll *never* come out of here."

"But you have to mommy! Please!"

"No! I'll never come out of this closet because if I come out, he's going to beat me."

"No, mommy, he's not. You *have* to come out! You *have* to come out for *me*!"

"Sweetheart, I love you, but I want you to leave from this closet. I want you to go out and have your own life, somewhere far away from this dark place full of evil, do you hear me?"

She didn't actually say that she was going to leave; she just sat there on the floor with me.

"Alright mommy. If you're going to stay in here, then *I'm* going to stay in here, too." And she just sat there with me in the darkened silence.

After some time, it must have become apparent to him that neither one of us had yet to come out of the bedroom. He must have finally gotten down from his violent high and realized the extent of the damage he had just done. I know this because he came and knocked (not beat) on the closet door and said, "I'm so sorry... I shouldn't have lost it like that."

I didn't answer.

"Please, forgive me."

I still didn't answer.

"*Please*, come out of there. I *promise* I won't hurt you anymore."

"Go away! That's what you say all the time."

"*Please*. You *have* to come out of there. If you don't come out now, you'll never come out and you'll stay in there forever."

I couldn't believe this. Words of wisdom from the same person who, moments earlier, was about to kill me.

"You cannot continue to do this," I said in a voice I barely recognized as my own. I probably had trouble talking due to the blood I was still swallowing from my lip.

"I *promise* you I won't do this. But you have to come out. I'm going to open the door, and I want you to step out."

His opening the door didn't open up my heart to believe one word that came out of his cursed mouth. He had to literally step away from the door, and out of my line of sight, in order for me to even consider leaving the room. My daughter had to walk outside and tell me "Mommy, it's ok, you can come now," just to get me to leave.

Believe me all I wanted to do was to stay in that room and cry. I couldn't believe that this was all that my life had become. Here I was at 32 years old, and all I had to show for myself was *this*.

All the hope and promise I once held had been seized up by this unthinkable, inescapable nightmare that was represented by this closet. I had become so fearful of my own life that I dreaded stepping out of a little walk-in closet, so afraid that I would lose my life, in my own home at that. And my life would be lost, not to an intruder or a thief in the night but, to the person I was *married* to, the person with whom I had taken the very solemn vow of 'til death do we part.' It seemed to me that death would be the only thing to part us.

6
Nothing

Looking back over the events that made up my life at that time, one thing was always made clear: I was literally walking through a fire, and my survival relied upon my ability to withstand, and eventually exterminate, that fire.

In the summer of 1998, Florida was literally burning. Wildfires were incinerating much of the northern part of the state. You would think this wouldn't be an opportune time to drive, but *he* wouldn't think so.

We were on the road returning from a trip to New York. The smoke billowing from the fires in Central Florida could be seen from miles away in Jacksonville, in the northern part of the State.

On the drive home from New York, after stopping in South Carolina I had asked *Sam* to fill the tank up on our way down, but he insisted that we had more than enough gas to make it home, despite being over 300 miles away. I didn't think so, but in this marriage, my thoughts weren't worth anything. So as we journeyed closer to home, the gas needle remained dangerously close to empty.

Upon arriving in Jacksonville, the state troopers were redirecting all traffic. We were journeying south along Interstate 95 but would join Interstate 4 from Daytona Beach to Orlando. The state trooper did tell us to ensure that we had a full tank of gas as all gas stations along the interstate were closed due to the fires. It goes without saying that he did not heed the advice of the trooper.

The smoke was so thick that it made what would usually be a sunny evening look like midnight, severely decreasing our visibility. In those conditions, it would have been easy to become disoriented and to have a fatal accident. To make matters worse, the gas tank needle was inching closer to E. And the closer we got to home, the more the smoke thickened and the more intense the fires became.

After a while of driving, it became clear that we needed to get off the highway as soon as possible. State troopers and emergency personnel were posted along the route to make sure traffic kept moving. As we drove through, the wildfires raging in the median and on both sides of the highway was just like the fire that I lived through. I realized that my life in this fiery furnace of a marriage could be consumed if I didn't do something about it.

The fire that so consumed much of the state, killing innocent wildlife and scalding buildings, was now on either side of the freeway we were driving on. The flames danced and flickered this way and that, eating up everything in their path. Their reddish, orange color seemed mocking in a sort of way; while the fire blazed with such vibrant life, everything it so much as touched was rendered dead and gone. *If this is what hell is like, it's a place I sure don't want to go.*

The heat from the blaze was sweltering, to say the least. It felt as though the heat had traveled through the atmosphere, seeking me out, saving its worst most tormenting affects just for me. I imagined what that fire would feel like licking up my bones the way it was licking up everything in its destructive path. Would the heat be so hot that it became ice cold and turned into white heat? Would my death be quick? Or would I slowly broil and burn to my agonizing end? The only comfort I received at this point was imagining what it would be like if *he* slowly broiled and burned to an agonizing death.

I had already been begging him to stop the car and pull off the highway so we could refuel. I had already pleaded with him to take each and every exit we passed as to escape this earthly hell. I even tried to bargain with him; it seemed as though he wanted us to perish in the fiery furnace. It became apparent to me that Sam intended for us to run out of gas, and be left stranded on the side of the highway, with raging fires on either side. Obviously he didn't care for his life; I knew he didn't care about mine.

Who was I to ask such useless, stupid questions? Who was *he* to take heed of any common sense?

"Shut your damn mouth," he told me. "You haven't been driving for as long as I have so you don't know what the hell you're talking about." *Yeah, sure I don't.*

Alex began crying. She, too, beseeched him to come off the highway and to listen to mommy. He repeated to her the exact same thing he told me.

Despondent and certain that our fiery deaths were near, and not knowing what else to do, we began to pray. She and I, both of us sitting in the back seat, held hands and prayed like we'd never prayed before. Our very lives depended on it. As I prayed, I thought perhaps God would see me burning in this fiery hell and have mercy upon me; that he would reach down and pull me and my daughter out, leaving *him* to perish eternally in this blaze. As I looked around me and heard the chimes of the car signaling low fuel, I realized that Sam did not intend to stop.

I compared the fires we were driving through to the fires that I experienced in our home and I cannot forget the sight of the fires burning in the median and on either side of the freeway. I cannot forget the terror and helplessness I felt as I realized that the charming man I had married had become a monster whose sole purpose was to destroy me. I realized that I know what prison feels like. I didn't have to sit behind bars to experience it. I was living it day in day out being married to a man, trapped inside the fiery furnace of a marriage. For the first time I wondered if this is what would be the end.

Would my innocent child and I really have to be consumed in a fiery furnace due to a man's sheer stubbornness and refusal to heed warnings? Is five the only age she would ever be allowed to see? What kind of *monster* had I married who would willingly endanger the lives of his family?

When we reached the junction, the fire was now blazing through the median and the highway was reduced to two lanes in both directions. By this time the state troopers were directing the traffic and telling everyone to keep on driving and, whatever happened, to *not* stop or pull over, and to also keep our windows up. They had placed orange cones on the road to direct drivers, as there was very low visibility. Because *he* was a speed demon, he became disoriented and started bumping through the orange cones. He nearly lost control of the vehicle.

I was a hysterical mess at this point. Sam did not heed warnings to turn off the air conditioning, as the smoke was pulled in through the air system. Between tears of fear, I tried again to convince him to take the next exit. To my surprise he listened, but not in the way I wanted him to. He pulled over to the shoulder, put the car in 'park', turned to me and spat "*You* drive." Then he reclined the seat, strapped his seat belt on, put on his sunglasses, and turned to look at me.

When I went behind the wheel, the gas needle was below E, the red light next to the gas indicator was flashing bright red, same as the color of the flames tearing up the median, and the warning sound indicating low fuel was ringing; in my ears, it felt more like someone scratching their nails down a dry blackboard over and over and over again. I thought to myself *Lord, if you took us this far, surely you will not leave us.*

As I pulled into the speeding traffic, I realized with great horror that not only was there fire eating up the median; there was now fire on either side of the freeway, the same as before. Now the likelihood of my perishing was tripled. *If I have to die, does it have to be at the same time* he *dies? How unfair!*

As carefully as I could (as careful as one can be driving a car with the gas needle on 'empty' and with fire and smoke blazing for as far as the eye can see), I navigated through the traffic and the fire without incident. About five miles into my driving, I spotted an exit. I thanked my lucky stars and pulled off. Of course, *he* didn't think there was any reason to come off the highway because he was enjoying the heat; he had his seat reclined and his sunglasses on, ready to die in style.

As I climbed onto the exit ramp, there was a gas station with one light on. The state trooper's words about there not being any open gas stations replayed through my head, but nonetheless, I thought, what the heck; living in this marriage had given me as many near-death experiences as one can have in a lifetime. Why not take one more chance now? I parked the car and walked in.

There were only two people there, and they were both behind the counter. Most of the lights in the station had been shut off and even the low buzzing sound that accompanies the coolers in a gas station was absent. I assumed that the two men standing behind the counter were the owners, and I was right.

One of them looked up at me and smiled and said, "I *knew* I was waiting on someone. I had been warned by everybody to shut down the station and leave *hours* ago, but I just couldn't do it." And there I was, the answer to his hesitation to leave. He quickly filled up our gas tank, told us the safest driving routes, and wished us all good night.

When I finally got home that night, I was too tired to even *think* about dragging our bags from the car to the house. I, instead, went straight into Alex's room and sat with her in silence. Words weren't necessary between us, as what we had just experienced didn't require them. While *he* slept ever so peacefully on the couch, my little angel and I sat on her bed, held hands, and thanked God that we were both alive.

My marriage had become a firestorm of physical and emotional abuse that was so potent it made me feel as though my very existence was defined by the violence that existed in our home. There appeared to be no reasonable means of liberation from the firestorm without leaving behind a significant part of myself. There seemed to be no end in sight.

I made up in my mind that through the fire, I will walk. If it means that I will have my daughter with me at the end, then so be it. I was now convinced that her life would be at its best if she lived with me rather than living with her father.

I had seen how, over time, he was capable of attempting to control her mind and her emotions against me. Had she not had positive experiences of being with me, it's fair to say that she would have believed her mother was a no-good, low-down person, just as her father always described me. But because I continually poured out my love to her, and because she was constantly affirmed when in my presence, she made the realization that her mother is a good person, and that she, too, would walk with her through the fire. She would often tell me, in that angelic voice of hers, that I was a good person, and one day, we're going to get out of this.

That alone was enough for *him* to spark up a 'competition' to see whom she would love the most. But she had already made up in her mind that while she loved her daddy, she loved her mommy more because her mommy was hurting because of all the bad things that daddy did.

It seemed that his bouts of violence always occurred on days following nights when I had fitful sleeps and bad dreams. There was even a pattern to the nightmares. Alligators, wolves and snakes, any animal that terrified me and made me shake down to my core were always chasing me. During the following day, the bad dreams would become a bad reality, except it wasn't an alligator or a snake hunting me, but instead, my own husband.

This night, I dreamt that an alligator was chasing me. But this alligator ended up morphing into my husband. I woke up trembling.

The situation within our marriage had deteriorated to the point where we no longer slept in the same bed, nor did we sleep in the same room. He had a penchant for staying up throughout the nights. Because I was the working spouse, I couldn't afford this luxury. So he would sleep on the couch in the family room and watch TV all night. He would turn the TV up to a deafening volume that made it uncomfortable for anyone else in the house to sleep. So not only was I tormented by nightmares, but I was also disturbed by the ear-splitting volume of the TV. Any attempts to turn it down or ask him to do so sparked an argument. To avoid arguments and beatings, I usually left the subject alone.

But this night, it felt as though I was walking on hot coals. This day was no different from other mornings. When I got up, he immediately set the stage for what would decline into severe emotional abuse. At the end of that would come the physical part of the abuse.

The night before, he had been throwing around comments and phrases, but I ignored them. I turned to my usual form of escape: writing. If I could not write at a time I wanted to write, I would watch soothing inspirational stories on TV. The stories helped me to temporarily forget the hellhole that I lived in.

He liked to use our daughter as a means of getting me to talk to him (because I usually never held casual conversation with him). Before I fell asleep, he had told me that I was spoiling her because I allowed her to sleep in the chair next to my bed, and that I should let her sleep in her room. The best part of the night was during the first two hours when I fell asleep. In that deep sleep, the roar of the TV didn't bother me. But as the night dragged on, I became more tormented. After a while, I gave up on sleeping altogether.

At the time, I had a job as an entry-level cashier at a supermarket. And he *reveled* in that, how it was such a comedown and a downgrade for me to work in this lowly position. He now felt that he was in charge.

This day, I was off from work, and he came home after his usual morning routine of dropping our daughter at school. After the way he carried on the night before, I was hoping nothing would come out of it. I knew that wouldn't be the case.

As soon as he walked in the door, he said, "You know things have to change around here."

That sentence always prefaced anything that was going to go wrong. It was as if he were God decreeing what was going to happen in my life; in my opinion, only God could make a pronouncement like that.

My usual response was never intended to provoke him, but with his countenance, much wasn't needed to provoke him at all.

"Ok," I said gently.

"What? You don't have anything to say? You think you're better than me? Why don't you have something to say?"

"Ok. What more could I have said?"

"*What more could you have said?* See, that, there? You have a smart mouth! Everything I say, you have to say something about it. *I'm* the man around here! *I* wear the pants, not you!"

"Yes, you do wear the pants…*you* are the man." I was doing everything in my power to keep him from exploding; agreeing with him seemed like an easy choice. I was wrong.

"What are you trying to say?"

"I'm not trying to say anything." I thought to myself, *why don't you shut up?* So I stopped speaking.

He went and sat before the TV to continue his tirade.

"That's the problem with you. You just have too much mouth. You think you're better than me! What makes you think you're better than me? This is *my* country. *I'm* in charge. If I don't do anything for you, you won't be anything, you understand? You're *nobody!* You're *nothing!*"

I just stood there and continued to wash the dishes in the sink in silence. I had a good feeling as to where this was going. And I was right.

"You're *nobody*! You're *nothing!*" he repeated. "When I met you, you were *nothing*. And now you're *nothing*. I brought you here to make you somebody, but now I see that you're *nothing* but low trash! *Nothing!*"

"I agree with you; I really am nothing. Yes, certainly, if that's how you feel."

"Yeah you *better* agree with me! Because if it weren't for me, you'd be full of trash and be absolutely *nothing*! You're nothing but an old piece of trash somebody left on the side of the street. If I hadn't picked you up off the side of the street, then you'd be *nothing!*"

Is he suffering from delusions of grandeur? I thought to myself. *What street corner did this man find me on and precisely when did he 'pick me up?'* He must have heard me think it because his next words were "What are you *trying* to say? You think you're better than me! You think because you were working in an office that you're better than me? Look at you now! Look at what you are! Now you have to work as *cashier* and stand behind a counter and ring up stuff. You think you're anybody now? Look what you have become? Look at how you've come down in life?

What are you going to do now? Go ahead and call your friends. There! Pick up the phone and call one of your powerful, influential friends! Let's see where that will get you now!"

  I was just standing at the counter wiping the sink over and over again. It was important that I not internalize any of the vicious words that were coming out of his mouth. I had to pretend that it was happening to someone else and that I was dreaming about it. In my mind, I would pretend I was on seashore somewhere and looking out at the ocean. Wiping the sink with a dry cloth produced that calming effect in me. Not only would I not remember, I wouldn't respond either. That in itself provoked him. To him, it was symptomatic of my condition; in his mind, my condition was that I believed that I was better than him, and as such, I didn't see it fit to answer him. How *stupid* logic is that? It was at times like these that I would retreat into that imagery, where I was sitting on seashore, watching the waves roll in and out. Alex used to say that it was at the worst times of the emotional and mental abuse that I would sit perfectly still. She described it as I would sit as still as a stone. It was my way of not allowing any negative thoughts and emotions from penetrating my consciousness.

  As I dried the sink over and over, he said, "What are you doing standing there, wiping the sink? Don't you have anything else to do?"

I knew what that meant. He was sending me away from a place where I had numerous exits (in the kitchen) and to a place where he could corner me to have me at his mercy - the bedroom.

I didn't know what to do. I looked down at myself, and as is typical for southern summer weather, I was dressed in shorts and tank top. I would usually be wearing long-sleeved shirts and pants that would act as a buffer between his fists and my delicate skin; the cuts, scratches and bruises didn't show through clothes that covered them up. This soon-to-be-attack caught me completely off guard.

The next thing I knew he was standing right in front of me. He grabbed me at my throat and said, "Did you hear what I said? I said *what are you doing standing here?*"

"Please, please, I *beg* you, please…" I didn't recognize my own voice due to the tremors that racked through it.

"Bow down to me! I am your GOD!"

"There really is no need to do this, please… I haven't done anything…"

"What do you *mean* you haven't done anything? You have done *more* than enough! Didn't I tell you that you *never* should look at me like that?"

How did I look at him? I'm quite sure the only thing being conveyed through my eyes was paralytic fear.

"Didn't I tell you never look at me from under your eyes like you're *better* than me?"

While holding my throat, he pushed me through the dining room. By this time, I was so terrified. I couldn't say anything. I couldn't scream. I couldn't shout.

The subdivision we lived in was partially unfinished. Because of this, there was some construction going on next door. I suddenly realized that the hammering and loud construction noises had stopped. But I didn't think the sudden quiet had anything to do with me.

By this point, he was yelling at the stop of his lungs, consumed by his rage. His eyes were bulging out of his head. One hand was tightly gripping my throat and the other hand was in a balled up fist, ready to come.

He pushed me into the bedroom. I knew if I went in there, it was over. I knew this time, there would be no escaping and I would surely be dead at the end of it. As he pushed me into the bedroom, I grabbed the doorpost and refused to go any further.

That's when the first fist came and I ducked. I ran back into the living room. As I ran into the living room, I tumbled over the coffee table, dumping one of the ornaments onto the floor. He grabbed my leg and I took the ornament and swung around trying to swipe at him. That infuriated him even more.

I tried to run to the front door to open it and he caught me before I could and slammed me up against it. He tried to grab at me again, but I ran through the family room, through the narrow passageway, and came back. He caught me. I was like a pent animal. He knew that as long as he was blocking the front door, I couldn't get out. When I tried to run through the garage door, I realized that he had already locked it.

He had me penned. I ran around back into the living room, desperate to get out of there. I tried to go through the sliding door in the family room, but he had jammed it with a picture frame.

He hauled me back into the living room by my hair with me kicking and screaming. He slammed me against the wall, picked me up, opened his balled up fist and slapped me across my face. My head twisted sideways. I felt as though I had lost every last tooth in my mouth. He slapped me so hard that I saw the sun, the moon, the stars and all the galaxies in between. I thought my head had completely come off my body with the force of this 230-pound man slapping me.

When I finally realized that I could move my head, he was holding my head and slapping it against the wall. I finally started screaming as loud as my vocal chords could go and the scream paralyzed him. In those few seconds of opportunity, I ran from out of his grasp, threw open the front door, and ran outside.

When I ran outside, I realized why the construction workers had stopped hammering. They had been working on the house next door for some time, and had become aware to the abuse that went on during the daytime. As soon as I ran out, one of them shouted across the lawn "Are you ok, ma'am?"

I couldn't say anything.

The neighbors who were across the street had called the police. One of them said, "Ma'am, we've called the police and help is on the way."

That was all it took to make me break down. Tears poured out of my eyes like never-ending rivers.

I had not realized that Sam also came outside. One of the construction workers said to him, "Sir, we've been here for a while now. And we're not telling you how to live your life, but if you *touch* her again, we *promise* you that you're going to feel it."

When the dispatched police came, the officer walked me to the end of the driveway, and he said, "Ma'am, you *don't have to live in this*. Do you have anyone you can go to? You can't continue to stay in this."

By this time, Sam walked back into the house, went into the bathroom, and used his razor to cut his face. He came back out and told the police officer that he hit me in self-defense because I cut his face with the razor.

The police officer said to him "Sir, you want to tell me how a 5'1, 125-pound woman can cut up a big guy like you with a razor? Come on!"

The police called Sally who came as quickly as she could. In the meantime, with the police present, I went inside the house and then packed an overnight bag. Next, Sally took me, and Alex, away from the house.

When I got to Sally's house, she told me that I had to go to the bathroom and then look at myself. I refused to look in the mirror because I could not look at my face knowing what had just been done to me. I didn't want to confront it. But she said that I *had* to.

I went to the bathroom. When I got there, I had a weird sense of déjà vu, as though I had already been here. As I looked around her guest bathroom walls, I realized why. The color of the walls was the same walls that I had seen in my dream the night before. I had dreamt I would be in her bathroom, and here I was, the next day, as a result of the abuse.

Alex and I were ensconced at her house and we were staying there until we could find a way out. As a result of the police activity, we had to provide them with a forwarding address. They suggested I obtain an injunction against him so that it would keep him away from me.

Sally was a new friend and because I hadn't known her for a long time, I was unsure as to how long the living arrangement was going to last. I didn't want to impose on her, but I didn't have a choice. She gave us permission to stay for a few days until I could figure out what would happen next.

Once I obtained the police report, I had to now file an injunction for protection. This was my first encounter with the judicial system. In the meantime, I had to figure out how I was going to get Alex to school.

Children have a funny sense of pride. One of Alex's friends lived down the street from our house and also attended the same school. Living in a nice family, where it seemed we shared some things in common, the youngest had been very friendly to Alex. We never got to know them, as Sam did not want any contact with anyone he did not choose. Alex was not allowed to go, and play as much as she wanted to play, with the family because that was one of *his* rules.

Before this incident happened, the father of my daughter's friend came over to our house. "Why won't you let the children play?" he had asked Sam.

No response.

The man said, "Do you have something against my family?"

"No, of course I don't have anything against you. There's nothing wrong." Of course, this was his nice-guy, friendly neighbor role.

"Then why won't you let the child come out and play? Let her come out and play with my daughter. And why won't you let your wife talk to my wife? They're women, they can go out and go shopping together."

He was ambiguous in his answer, again. The man seemed to be silently communicating that he knew what was going on in the home, as if he knew that socializing with his wife would be

Sam relinquishing control over me. He was communicating with Sam in a way that threatened *him*, but didn't threaten me at all.

One day when I walked down to his house, he asked me if I had any family at all. My standard answer was no, of course; my nearest family lived 1,500 miles away. His next words were so specific, I'll never forget them: "Ok. I don't know how, but it's all going to work out and you and your daughter will be ok."

During the time I stayed at Sally's house, I was terrified of sending Alex to school because I thought that *he* would try to come and pick her up from school and I would never see her again. I called a friend, Daisy who lived in the next town and who had been Sam's childhood friend. I asked if we could come stay with her and enroll Alex in a school near where she was because I was sure that given opportunity, *he* would take her away.

Whenever I did take my little angel to school, I would call the police to escort me there for protection. When it was time for school to be dismissed, the police were there to make sure he didn't come and pick her up. And you'd better believe that *he* was there at exactly 2:30 in the afternoon to get her.

I called the school and notified them of the situation and the teacher was compassionate enough to keep my daughter in the classroom (even after dismissal) until *I* walked in there to pick her up. That process (dropping her off and picking her up with the aid of Sally and the protection of the police) continued for a few days until I worked it out.

The next day, I went to the courthouse to file an injunction for protection from him. When I filed it, he was served with notice and he had to appear. The injunction was granted and I had to appear in court to testify against him.

He told the court that *I* was the bad parent and the worst mother. He told them I was an illegal alien who had no right to be here and that because *he* was a citizen, I shouldn't have any rights to my own child.

The judge, who I thought would take his side because he played the part of the choirboy so well, was surprisingly indifferent towards him. "Well, her citizenship is not our concern nor is it a matter for us to decide," he spoke in a raspy voice. "The fact of the matter is, sir, that regardless of your citizenship, *you* hit her, and according to the police report, the neighbors say that you violently abused her over time. Based on that, she's attempting to start her life over. The court is thereby granting the injunction based on that." That was more than enough for me. But it wasn't enough for *him*.

Would you believe Sam countered by filing an injunction against *me*? The abuser trying to protect himself from the abused; how silly does that sound? He alleged that *I* abused *him* physically. I honestly think if I had the physical strength to abuse him in any way, he would have been a dead man at that point.

So *I* had to go to court to testify of my innocence and say that I did not scratch him because I didn't wear long, artificial nails nor did I have the strength to do such a thing. Once my injunction against him was granted, he was ordered to not come within 500 feet of me. The matter of visitation and custody was a task relegated to the family court.

Alex and I temporarily moved to another friend's home, which was in fact his friend Daisy. Daisy and her family provided us shelter and food. Daisy also tried to get me another job. At this point, I couldn't return to my job as a cashier because *everybody* there heard about what happened. The day after the incident, I had to call in to say why I wasn't going to return. All of my co-workers and employers now knew that *he* had beaten me within an inch of my life.

The first thing Daisy suggested was retail therapy. You can imagine that at this point, I didn't have a penny to my name because all my money was placed in a joint account that *he* used, claiming he was paying bills. What he was really using it for was his gambling problem; he would take the money I earned and throw it down the drain (or, more accurately, at the convenience store, buying lottery tickets).

Of course, he never won, not even *one* red cent, from that stupid addiction. As much money went into the account from my job was as much money as he took out. Our monthly expenses were not much to begin with, because we owned the house we lived in, and he owned his car; all we had to pay were utilities. For any other person, that life would have been a dream. For me, it was living hell.

I didn't have much, if any, say in the matter. I had tried to open an account, but that went disastrously wrong, as evidenced by my current living situation.

As soon as I went to the mall with my friend, I started looking for a job more than I looked for clothes or trinkets. If anyone knows anything about working in a mall is that you usually have to start out in retail working at a cosmetics counter before you advance any further.

Because I found solace at the mall and at all the other shopping centers we went to, I can now say God bless the person who created shopping centers and God bless retail therapy.

The ability to go out, walk around, mingle with other people, to be perfectly normal without fear of punishment, and to do it all with my Alex, was a pleasure I hadn't experienced in a long time. Even if only for a little while, I was able to forget the abuse. I was able to freely imagine what it would be like to live like the people I saw mingling around, to live normally and to live in perfect peace. What a gift that was.

As I was walking around the mall, I went into a large department store and inquired as to whether I could get a job there. They had me fill out a form and told me they would contact me if they were interested.

This entire arrangement (enrolling Alex in a nearby school, living with a friend, looking for a job) lasted all of two months. Then *Sam* decided that it was time for his wife and daughter to come home. He knew where we were staying because there were only so many people I knew; most of the people were *his* friends anyway.

He called Daisy and started badgering her with the Nice-Guy Guilt Trip. He was so sorry, he couldn't live with himself and what he had done to his family, he wanted his family home so badly and how he would do *anything* to see the face of his daughter again, etc. Daisy believed strongly in the institution of marriage even if it eventually cost your life. She believed once you were married, you should *stay* married, no matter what the cost.

She never talked about the abuse with me, even though I told her about it. She never said that *he* was wrong for what he did and she never told me I was doing the right thing, either. Unknown to me, Alex had been complaining to her, and to another friend of mine, that they had to help her mommy because her daddy was going to kill her mommy. And still Daisy did nothing. By her silence she was complacent with it. What should I have expected? She was his friend, after all.

Imagine that - a small child begging for outside help and explaining the nightmare she and her mommy were living at home.

But they were *his* friends, so they *never*, not even *once*, made any attempt to tell him that he was wrong. They never told him *you shouldn't have*. They gave him no reason to stop doing what he was doing: no reprimands, no threats, *nothing*. But thankfully, Daisy allowed me to stay with her and her family, who helped me with transportation, as I didn't have a car of my own.

Now that I look back on it, it was all a setup, really. She gave me just enough resources and access to whatever I needed to make the situation halfway decent. But she also restricted me from certain freedoms so I would become desperate for my *own* freedom and be willing to do whatever it took to get my freedom and my peace back. In other words, she made it so that I would have no choice but to go back to *him*.

Apparently, *his* daily guilt trips on her were beginning to wear her down, because she bought his story. She believed that he was sorry and that he was truly repentant. It didn't matter that, for three weeks, I *still* had the black and blue bruises and I *still* had the scratches and scars to prove his viciousness. It didn't matter how many times Alex pleaded with her to not let us go back or how many times she had to repeat the horror stories of what she saw her daddy do to her mommy. As long as *he* was her friend, none of that counted. She just believed things like this happened in marriages all the time and it was just a matter of both of them working it out for the better. The better meant staying married, no matter what cost.

Daisy's husband warned her to not get involved. But he did tell her that if she *could* help me, then she *should*. And he told her to not send me back.

We spent some time shuffling between Daisy and her daughter's house, and by this time, Alex was attending school regularly. Alex had always been a bright student (she was always placed in the advanced classes and one time was offered the opportunity to skip a grade). That in itself was a testimony to her excellent academic ability. Despite the uncertainty of her home situation, she did not let her grades suffer. In fact, her grades skyrocketed even further during this time. She had no emotional stability in her home (she didn't even really have a home) and she had no peace. She never knew from one moment to the next if she was going to see her mommy alive or in a body bag on the way to the coroner's office. But, nonetheless, she still maintained her grades and her intelligence.

You can only stay with friends for so long, because after a while, you start wearing out your welcome. My time with them was up. It became apparent that *he* not only wore down their defenses, but he wore mine down as well. I was completely dependent on Daisy's system of transportation to get to and from work, and I was completely dependent on her daughter, Sadie, getting Alex back and forth to school (I was using Sadie's address for the school bus to pick her up).

Daisy started to display her 'bad face' and subtly began letting me know that it was time to leave. She would drop comments like "Maybe it's time for you to go back to your home" and "These things happen in marriages" and "Spouses belong *together*". And boy did she ever use the Bible as her final authority: "The Bible says that a woman should submit to a man, and a woman's place is in her home and with her husband."

I knew exactly what that meant. By this time, *Sam* had all but perfected his role as a loving, caring husband desperate to make amends with his family. He made it seem as though he'd done nothing wrong and that I left him foolishly and without cause. Every day, he called to ensure that I was ok and that his daughter was being well taken care of. He would always say how much he missed us and how he wished we would come back because he was so lonely and so in need of our love.

I was barely hanging on to the little job that I had because the Daisy who was responsible for my transportation, in an effort to make her point clear about how I should go back home, became purposefully unreliable.

The one time I spoke to him when he called, he was nothing but apologetic and love and tender care. He told me how he and our child were all that he had in this world and that he was *nothing* without us. He told me how it was his fault that I was in this position and he was the cause of all my troubles.

"Just allow me to help you. Now that you have a job, we can work something out together, if you would only let me help you and make up for everything I've done..." He sounded so truthful, so innocent and so right.

I had no other choice but to go back to the abuse I was running from. I had no help, no money, and no means of empowerment. I couldn't work long enough hours to save up enough money because of an unreliable means of transportation. Without working, I couldn't save enough money to permanently remove myself from the situation.

The most intrinsic thing was that I had no support. If I had a support system, and a *willing* support system to help, then I would have become more empowered.

Not really believing the situation was going to heal on it's own, like so many people around me said, and with great trepidation, I said *one last time I am going back into this situation. And if I ever have to come out again, that will be the* very last *time I'll have to do so.*

He promised the sun, the moon, the stars and all the galaxies in between. He promised that things would change for the better. He even suggested that we should move to a town closer to the city so I could get a better job.

Before I had been rudely pushed out of my home, I had applied everywhere for a job. I wasn't satisfied with just working as a cashier in a supermarket. But a new shattering revelation would come to me sooner than I imagined.

7
Promises & The Lion's Mouth

When I moved back home, I found out most of the places I had applied for work had actually responded. People had called saying they were interested in interviewing me because I was qualified. One company, in particular, had offered a well-paying position that also provided benefits and flexible hours, and they had called back saying they wanted me to take the job. But when they called, *Sam* answered and told them I had moved out of town and had left the state.

I found this out the very same day I moved back. He had been kind enough to let me get the mail this time. When I got the mail, I took the envelope that was addressed to me, and opened it. The letter said that the company had been trying to reach me for weeks on end to give me the position I so desperately needed. They went on to say that the man who answers the phone claiming to be your husband told us that you had moved away permanently.

I was rendered speechless and stunned. I couldn't believe the cruel irony in the situation, the irony being that the very same day I move back home is the very same day I find out that *he* is still up to his old, wicked tricks.

Confounded, I turned to him and said, "How could you? You know how *desperately* I – we – needed this job. How could you have said something like that? *Why* would you say something like that?"

"Well, I didn't say those specific words..."

Liar, liar, pants on fire, I thought hurtfully. They were all lies. Just like the lies he said when he *promised* that he would never hit me again, *promised* he would never put me in a position like that again, *promised* I would never again have anything to fear.

I guess when they said promises are like babies (easy to make but hard to deliver), they must have been speaking from experience.

Because this smooth-talking monster had *promised* me he wouldn't take advantage of my vulnerabilities, such as my lack of documentation and lack of support from any nearby family or friends. *So you already took advantage of those things. Now you take advantage of my economic situation as well?*

I now think there is a *special* place in Hell reserved *just* for him. That Satan himself sits on his fiery throne, *waiting* for the day when he will meet his most abominable creation: *him.* I sometimes even wonder if Hell will be too good a place for him; that maybe even Lucifer, the Death

Angel, will think his ways too nefarious, and spit him right back out. Where will he go then?

As I read the letter, I put it down and said "Now what?"

Sam had answer even for that: "Now you can go get another job. And let's go see about getting you a car because it's time you had one."

A car, I thought. *Wow! What a novel thought, is it possible that freedom is in sight?*

I went back to the big department store I'd applied to (and been dutifully ignored by) and went up to the woman who had received my application. With my back up against the wall and with me shoved into a corner, I became the kind of woman I one day dreamt of being.

"I don't care if it takes me all night or if it takes all day," I growled, looking at her in her eyes. "I'm going to sit right here all night if I have until you *give* me a job."

That seemed to work. I was hired on the spot. Relief, right? Ha! You know the answer.

They paid me minimum wage, which means I barely managed to meet my expenses. The good thing, and there were many good things, was it gave me freedom from the physical and emotional violence which was taking place in my home daily.

I loved my new job and my co-workers welcomed me. I was about to finally enjoy some freedom and peace of mind, being away from all that negativity and tension that defined my daily existence; finally I was able to breathe. This could be the peace I was asking for, the freedom and ability to think and hear myself think. The one thing the tension and abuse took away from me was my 'peace of mind'. I couldn't think as long as I was being tortured on a daily basis. And if I couldn't think, how could I plan to get away?

Abuse not only shatters you physically, but the internal destruction and damage to your self-esteem is really what ultimately destroys you. If you allow yourself to start listening to the lies told about you, by the person who is abusing you, you begin to believe them and you stop trying. You literally quit thinking and you start seeing yourself as his words define you. You have to learn to find peace in the midst of the storm raging around you and locate that peace whatever source it comes from to you and hang on to it, as it will help you to keep your mind together.

Many days I would sit as still as a stone while being mentally and emotionally demeaned, and I literally would allow my mind to tune out his words. My mind would take me to a peaceful state. This allowed me to survive the extreme mental and physical violence I had to live through.

This is why the price of my freedom was bought at the expense of not losing my mind. When it was over and all said and done, I lost a house, money, and my daughter's college fund. But the one thing that I kept was the freedom to have and enjoy my peace of mind.

That low-paying job became the stepping-stone to my freedom. It was the tool of economic empowerment that motored me towards achieving my ultimate freedom from emotional and physical violence. That job allowed me to be as far away from the abuse as I could get. To be in an environment free from mental and physical abuse on a daily basis, I kissed the floor with gratefulness. Sometimes on my lunch breaks I would sit in the mall enjoying the ambience and relative freedom.

Watching other women and their children, I would sometimes daydream that I will have the same opportunity to be free and take my daughter to the mall. This is why to this day I believe in retail therapy, as an aid for all that ails you. I found Shopping Malls to be wondrous places where I was free, but for a few moments, from the disaster my life had become. Many days I would sit in my car in Mall parking lots, waiting to go home, enjoying moments of peace before facing what I knew to be the fiery furnace of my marriage.

It was a long commute to the job and it was summertime so Alex was home for vacation. I knew when she returned to school, the commute would present itself as a problem. For the first time in my marriage, I actually agreed with Sam and started asking around as to where I could get an affordable car.

Someone suggested that I go to an auto dealership in the neighboring town that was desperate to get cars off their lot, so desperate they would sell their cars to just about anyone, including those who had low-paying jobs and no credit like myself.

A friend referred me to a specific salesman, so I called him and he told me to head over to look at a car. When I got there, they were more than eager to sell their cars. I was thrilled when I found a car that I liked that was also reasonably priced. The salesman said all I would need is a co-borrower. My heart fell.

I couldn't think of anyone, besides the obvious, who could – *would* – cosign a loan. I certainly didn't think to ask *Sam* because buying a car would mean that I have more liberation and he has less control. And since he thought the world we lived in should revolve around him and him only, he would say no to that.

The salesman was a mature man, but a wise one. He said, "Let me ask you something. What exactly are you trying to do?"

"What do you mean?" I asked.

"It seems to me you need more than a car."

At the time, I *never* talked about the abuse, unless pressed to do so and only then to someone I trusted. Saying the word out loud was hard for me, even if I were talking about abuse in regards to someone else. I was unaware that my facial expression and body language communicated what I was trying to hide.

But the way he looked at me and read my face did more than words could have ever done in terms of explaining my situation.

"You know," he continued, "I have a daughter about your age. I'm thinking to myself that if she were in trouble, I would want someone, anyone, to help her in any way possible."

My heart leaped with hope. "Sir, if there's *anything* you can do to help me get this car, please, I ask you to help me. I am in *dire* need of this car."

"Here's what we'll do. We need to have a co-borrower, and your spouse is the only other person you know. When you go home, be nice to him. Tell him that getting the car means you'll help him pay the bills. Getting the car means he won't have to drive his precious car to drive you back and forth everywhere you need to go. Tell him that his car is going to acquire mileage, wear and tear driving you back and forth to the city every day. Then say that none of that will happen if you have your own car. And he won't ever have to worry about you messing up his ride again with groceries, food crumbs, spills, etc."

"Yeah," I said, my confidence gaining. "That's a good idea."

The plan was good because it appealed to every aspect of his demented personality. It put him back in the driver's seat and gave him the feeling of being in control; it would make him feel as though he were the judge again, giving him the authority to make the final decision.

I went home that night and as usual, his badgering began.

"You didn't get the car did you? I told you that you wouldn't get it," he snarled as soon as I walked in the door.

"Yeah, you know, you're right," I carefully began. I knew that with him, I had to tread carefully. "Those people are something else, man. The guy wouldn't even budge no matter how much I tried to reason and compromise!"

"Yeah, I told you that they're hard-assed. You see, *I* always end up being right. You should listen to me more often." I let him continue on like that until I thought he was done.

"Yeah, you know, they're trying to prevent me from earning some money."

This was the bait. Would he grab at it, like he'd grabbed at my throat so many times before? Or would he see through my ruse and choose to punish me accordingly?

"What do you mean?" he said. His interest was piqued.

"The thing is if I don't have a car, then I won't be able to work. If I don't work, then I don't have any money. Then we won't be able to go visit your friends because we won't have the money to do so. And you remember that nice shirt you saw at the store that you liked? If I had a car and was able to work with more stability, then you could have some extra cash to go and buy it."

"Oh," he said, the reasoning of my plan-sinking in. "So the salesman said that you can't get the car at all?"

"Well, he said I would need a co-signer on the loan to get the car, otherwise I can't get it all."

"Ok," he continued, "Where are you going to get the deposit?"

"The deposit?" I asked, playing dumb. "I really don't know what I'm going to do about that. I could use your help…"

"When you get the deposit, you come back and tell me. Then I'll think about maybe signing for it or not."

So it halfway worked. Now it was a matter of obtaining the depository fee and persuading him to co-sign. *Two down, one to go*, I thought.

The next day I called the salesman and told him that the plan had halfway worked; the only problem is that I need to have the deposit. Apparently he had a plan for everything, because he devised a strategy for me to obtain that too.

"I'm going to give you the name and number of someone I know," he said. "Go pay them a visit. And remember you only need $1,500 for the deposit. Nothing more, nothing less. If you take out a loan, you're probably going to pay them back at $50 a month. What you do is sign up for the automatic withdrawal payment plan so that every month, they withdraw the payment from your account. I already called Kathy at XYZ Finance Company and told her to expect you."

Those few sentences were like a healing salve to my wound. When I visited the woman, who was his friend, she proved herself to be as helpful as he had promised she would be. As soon as I walked in, she knew exactly who I was.

She sat me down and said, "I'm going to tell you something. This loan we're giving you, as a deposit for the car is one step closer to you obtaining your freedom. I want you to pay the money every month and eventually, you're going to pay it off. *Don't let* him *convince you to add more to the loan.* I'm warning you! We're going to ask for collateral. You're going to provide me a list of all the electronic equipment in your house. When you give me the list, I want him to sign it and bring it back."

So I called Sam and told him to bring the list to the Finance Company. When he got there, he was so rude and impolite that Kathy finally snapped at him that she didn't need his signature.

"I don't even have to give you the list with the stuff in my house! I'll just keep it to myself and you can go straight to hell!" I thought that surely Kathy would kick us both out and tell me to forget my chances of ever getting a car. But she didn't. She stuck to her guns. I started to believe that she had dealt with men like him before.

"Sir," she began in a condescending tone, "must I remind you that the items on that list are not yours alone? Half of them belong to your wife because you're both *married* to each other."

"So?" he asked bitterly.

"So," she returned, matching him in intimidation, "she's as much entitled to how it is disposed of as you are. *So*, I don't *need* your signature. And believe me *sir*, she's getting this check to walk out of here with today." Wow! I thought she is not afraid of him at all. Boy do I want to be like her.

Like she promised, right there in front of *him*, she made out a check to me for exactly the amount I needed for the deposit. And the check also covered the insurance deposit I needed for the car as well.

Sam was left with no choice but to let his mouth hang open in shock and awe of what just happened. I could tell by the look on his face that he had never been made an outright fool of, like that before, especially by a woman, and especially in public.

Sam drove me to the dealership so I could pay down on the car I wanted and take it home. He drove in complete silence, not even so much as a disgruntled huff.

By the time we had got to the dealership, Kathy had already called the salesman and informed him of the scene that just took place. The car I chose was beige 1999 Ford Escort. It was brand spanking new fresh off the assembly line.

Sam almost flipped a switch. When we got there, they had the car and keys ready to hand to me.

I gave the check to the salesman with victory on the horizon. Now all I needed was *his* signed name on the dotted line. When the salesman produced the document that required signature, *he* couldn't help but jump in with a snarky question.

"Is my credit going to be impaired because of this?" he demanded.

"No, nothing of yours is going to be affected by this," the salesman calmly answered. "Your signature just means you're the co-owner of the car. You're not responsible for any payments because the money is automatically withdrawn from her account every month. The amount she is to pay for the car is something she can afford based on her earnings; we have her pay stub to prove it."

"That's good because I don't want to be responsible for *anything*. If anything goes wrong or she misses a payment, it shows up on *her* credit, not mine." He was acting as though the decision was still left up to him.

"Yeah, you're right, actually," the salesman agreed. I looked at him and thought *why are you agreeing with this monster?* Then he winked at me. I got his plan immediately.

"Yeah, these women are something else," he continued, delving right into *his* weak spot. "I have a wife at home who knows how to spend money like it's going out of style and it always reflects on *my* credit. They just spend, spend, and spend without thinking about anyone but themselves. And they have the nerve to do it without even asking you first!" *You're good,* I thought.

His trap was well laid, because *Sam* played right into it like a fool. Even though it appeared as though things were going to work out for my good, I was still sitting there sweating bullets. *Would he just sign the thing already?*

Finally, after what seemed like eons of his tirades, he signed. When he did, the salesman sat back on his haunches and smiled.

"Ma'am, here is the key to your car," he said, happily handing me the keys to my new ride. "You're free to go."

He and I knew the real meanings behind his last phrase. I had finally extracted a victory out of the mouth of the lion.

8
Flesh

I'd been working for some time by now and I was enjoying it immensely. The initial euphoria of my new car and my new job had died down. Alex was back in her original school and her life had resumed with some level of normalcy. I had become accustomed to the varying shifts I worked in the department store. I was truly enjoying the freedom I found in going to work every day and choosing which hours I could work and whether or not I wanted to take the weekend shifts.

I was also enjoying socializing with other people on the job. Talking to people outside of my very limited world was such a thrill. Holding normal conversations with normal people was something I never had a chance to experience before I began working. This job was a blessing in disguise because it was far enough from home that it prevented *him* from driving there every hour of every day to check up on me. He couldn't because it was too far and he was too concerned with how much gas it would cost as well as the wear and tear on his car. That provided me with a blissful happiness and him with frustrated anger.

But even though he couldn't drive, he could call. And he did. *All* the time. Because I didn't have a cell phone yet, I had to provide him with my work number. It wasn't so much that I *had* to provide him with it as it was he *demanded* that I do so, and he did it under the 'just in case of an emergency' guise (seeing as how we had a small child in school). I knew that by giving him the number, I was giving up some my peace of mind, but I did it for the sake of my daughter so just in case there was an actual emergency, I could be found.

He would time me from the time I left home until I got to work. And if he called by the time I was *supposed* to reach work and I hadn't, I heard no end of it when I got home in the evenings. And then he would call me right before I was scheduled to leave, time me again and then repeat the same procedure. And, you know he called frequently during the day; God forbid I couldn't come to the phone because I was assisting a customer.

I did have a friend or two who were co-workers, and they became aware of his behavior. Once they knew I was being abused, they devised a system that whenever he called, if I didn't want to talk to him, they would tell him that I was with a customer, or that I was working the floor, or that I was in another unreachable part of the store. He couldn't yell or scream at them for obvious reasons. And if he became too persistent, they would become firm and threaten to call my supervisor. Whenever my supervisor spoke to him, she would tell him, in no uncertain terms, that I couldn't come to the phone because I was working. She'd also tell him to save whatever was so 'important' for when I got home. She also made sure to tell him that he wasn't to call there and hassle her staff any more. He got the message loud and clear.

That type of situation (where the rug of control is ripped out from underneath him) was something he had never dealt with before and it was something he didn't know how to handle. He didn't have anyone to push around anymore, so he would start to accuse me of being in 'cahoots' with them; that I was working with them to go against him. Exactly what we could have been working on is something that only existed in his imagination. His pattern of abuse began again, in earnest, because now he *needed* to prove to me that, ultimately, it was *he* who was in control.

As soon as I walked in the door from work, he would start. It would continue all through the evening, so I never got a chance to spend time with Alex, and it would carry on through the night, so I never received any sleep. The cycle would repeat it self when I woke up the next morning.

I remember waking up one night to use the bathroom only to find him sitting next to the bed.

"What are you doing?" I asked sleepily.

"I'm watching you," he responded coldly.

"Why?"

"Because I don't see you enough. You're always working and you can never answer the phone at work, so I don't know what you could be up to." I became aware that he was going through my underwear when I left it in the laundry. He did this to accuse me of 'whoring around' with the men I worked with. It makes you wonder where did he think I found the time to do this as he had me under his watch every minute of my day. He didn't get that his emotional and physical abuse made me afraid of intimacy with men. How could he be so blind not to see the effect the abuse had on my emotions. He deprived me of my self-esteem, depraved me of my emotions and then expected me to respond to emotional stimulation? What alternate universe did he live in?

What could I have 'been up to' when I was *working*? He made it sound as if I was planning a surprise attack or ambush on him, or that I was trying to rob him of something by not being at his beck and call every waking minute. And trust me when I say if I had the ability to plan an ambush on him, I would have done just that.

This pattern of abuse made me stay away at work a lot more. Even on days that I had off, I would still go in and work just so I wouldn't have to deal with him. This started to take its toll on my physical body because I would sometimes work seven days per week.

I thought a nice escape from this would be a whole day that Alex and I could have to us. We could go shopping, or go walking around in the downtown district, or go see a movie or go out to eat. I wanted to be able to take her out of that miserable environment, even if just for a day. More importantly, I wanted to be able to do things I'd seen other mothers do with their daughters that I longed to do with mine as well.

At work, I would see other mothers take their daughters to the different stores, and I would watch how they bonded, and how much fun they had together, and how they were creating memories that would one day be cherished by both of them. And I would sit there and watch them and wish with everything in me that I could do the same for my own child.

One night when I got home, I carefully broached the subject of having the day off the next day, and I gently suggested that I would like to take Alex to the mall.

"No." That was his answer, given before I could even finish my thought.

"Why?" I asked.

"Why do you want to take her to the mall? What are you and her going to at the mall? I want to come too."

"I want to take her to mall where I work."

"*Why* do you want to go *that* mall? Don't you see enough of it every day when you're so busy *working?*"

"Because that's where I work, so I can receive discounts on anything we buy. It would be a better choice financially."

No matter what I said, he flat-out refused.

I didn't know how else to convince him or to appeal to him. I couldn't spend any time with her without *him;* that was the bottom line.

While the physical abuse diminished, the verbal and emotional abuse skyrocketed. And the verbal/emotional abuse is just as bad as the physical. Now he didn't want to hit me because he was afraid the neighbors would call the police. In fact, he made sure he told me that I had 'set up' the neighbors against him and had told them lies about him. He even went as far as backing up this claim by saying that whenever he went outside to mow the lawn, no one would say hi to him, and no one spoke to him. And it was my entire fault. I had created this ugly scenario where I had lied to the entire world and told them that he was a bad man.

In his eyes, I was a wicked woman who told everyone what a horrible man he was. I made him look bad to his friends because now his friends didn't answer his calls or go out with him anymore.

"It's time for us to leave this neighborhood," was his declaration one day.

"Yeah, it's time," I agreed half-heartedly.

"It seems as though we can't live together anymore. Let's just get a divorce." My neck nearly snapped in two from the whiplash I received turning around to look at him. *Did I hear him right? Did he really just grant me my freedom?* Of course, I couldn't let on how excited I was, so I played it cool.

"Fine. I'll sign on the dotted line," was my detached answer. I wouldn't say that there were butterflies in my stomach; I would describe them more as kangaroos.

"But, wait a minute. You don't have your green card," he said. *Damn, he's right.*

"Don't worry about that," I retorted. "Let's just sign on the dotted line."

"Why don't we put the house on the market?" he suggested. *That's actually a good idea.* "If we put the house on the market, then we could make a killing off it, and we can both walk away happy."

"Whatever you agree is fine with me. If you feel this way, let's do it."

But the same man who was just about to grant us both our freedom from that pointless marriage was the same man who went back on every oath he had just made.

So I continued working, until they laid me off. But they gave me well-written referrals, so I looked for a replacement job.

I heard about a call center that was hiring. It was closer to home and it provided me with more pay and health benefits. My responsibility was to sit at a desk and answer phones for a cell phone company that operated out of the Mid-West.

They called me and told me that they were interested in hiring me. So I went in for the interview. I got the job.

When I started working there, the emotional abuse escalated even further. With this job, I was working longer hours and spending more time away from home. What I would do was take the later shifts; I would start at one in the afternoon. But I didn't let *him* know that.

To escape the reality of my existence, I would tell him that I was scheduled to be at work from 10 am and leave home by the time he dropped Alex off at school. To pass the time, I would go to a café and sit down to read a book, or I would go to work and sit in the break room hours before I was due to clock in. Sometimes I would go to the other stores that would open and just walk around aimlessly. I had no other reason in mind as to why I was doing this. I just needed some form of escape, no matter how temporary.

When I would become weary, I'd tell myself that I didn't have time to worry about being tired. I didn't have the luxury of staying home and resting because if I did that, I would be beaten. The only way to avoid physical confrontation was not to be there at all.

Because I had a cell phone now, he would try to call the cell phone when I was working. But I would tell him that I couldn't answer my cell phone at work because I wasn't allowed to. Then he figured the job was within driving distance, so he could drive during the day to 'visit' me. But the company provided security, protecting all of the perimeters of the building, as well as a manned, gated entry to the parking lot. In order to get in, you had to swipe your work ID. He could obtain a visitor's pass and enter the lobby of the building, but he couldn't come into the area where I worked. To him this was a barrier that prevented him from having access to me.

One time he came to my job and insisted that security let him through. The security guard told him it was a secured area and he wasn't allowed in. Then, Sam asked the man if I was there or not (as if the security guard would know, or care), and the security guard said he didn't know who I was because my face was just one face in a sea of hundreds that passed by him every day.

When I got home, that night, he proceeded to tell me about his 'encounter'. Then he had the nerve to say that because he couldn't actually *see* me working and because he couldn't *call* me to find out if I was working, he wasn't sure that I was even really *working* at all. Unbelievable. Just downright unfathomable.

He demanded that when I got to work, I was to call him from the work phone so that he would know that I really was where I said I was.

"You're just going to have to believe me when I tell you that I'm working. Why is that so hard to do? You see me bring home a pay check that pays the bills, don't you?" I was exasperated. But I saw an invisible light bulb go over his head.

"I know how I can make sure you're really working. I'll look at your pay stub and look at the hours that you clock in. *Then* I'll know for certain that you are where you say you are." He nodded his head, as though that idea made perfect sense

"How will that help?" I asked, stupefied.

"Well, if you're there for all those hours, then you'll be paid for all those hours, won't you?"

I could not believe the logic he was trying to insert in this clearly illogical and absurd plan.

I felt truly trapped at this point, trapped by a wicked man who had no intention of me ever gaining any personal freedom at all. What gave him the right to determine the personal liberties I could enjoy as an individual? Who made him lord and judge of my life?

I decided that I had no choice but to learn to live with it until I could find a way out of it with my life and my daughter's life intact. The company didn't mind that I clocked in hours before I was scheduled to work. Because my life was dependent upon how many hours I clocked in, I finally had to confess to my supervisor that I needed this job for reasons that extended far beyond the financial realm.

I earned heaps of money doing this. Through time, I earned more than enough to ensure a comfortable lifestyle. I didn't know this, but the Human Resources Officer and my supervisor, Cindy, had both been studying me closely since I had started working there. Cindy had taken a special interest in me and she had profiled my situation clearly from the beginning.

She knew, with just one look at me, what was going on at home.

I did find it strange that I had the freedom to come to work and stay for as long as I wanted to and still get paid for it. I had no idea that they took note of all the times I would spend waiting in the break room for my shift to begin, or all the times I would sit in my car in the parking lot waiting for the clock to strike one so I could start working. I just continued to work as much as I could.

Like I said before, *he* was afraid of hitting me now. His brush with the judicial system and the police officers scared his fists away from my body. Because I had taken his fists away, all he had left was his mouth. And boy, did he ever use that.

Doing everyday things like going grocery shopping by myself was a big problem. Even if it was just to pick up simple everyday items like milk, eggs, and cheese, he *had* to be there. And I couldn't use his money for groceries. So if Alex wanted something special or if I ran out of something at home, I'd have to get it on my own.

Once, on my day off, Alex asked for something for a school project. She insisted that we go on a Saturday because both she and I were off from school and work, and she wanted to choose it her self. Unknown to *him*, even though the company gave us one free weekend per month, I never took it. I didn't know what I would do for two whole days at home alone with the tyrant. In fact, I would tell him that my days off were staggered and far between, just so I wouldn't have to spend any number of consecutive days at home with him.

Everybody else in the company wanted their consecutive days and weekends off, everybody except for me.

Anyway, Alex said she needed something from the store that she needed for a special school project. And she insisted that I take her there on a day when we were both off. This day was a bright, clear Saturday. It was November, so the air was cool and crisp, and the summer heat was over.

It was such a nice day so the air conditioner had been turned off and I opened the door from the family room to the patio to let in some fresh air. Little did I know that would be the day my life would *almost* end.

I was sitting in the family room watching cartoons with Alex around midday. After watching a few cartoons, I mustered up courage to tell *him* that I wanted to go to the store with Alex. Expressly, I wanted to go to the store with *just* her.

When I stood before him and asked, he was sitting.

"I would like to take Alex to the store so we can spend some quality time together." He didn't say anything. He didn't even so much as move or look at me. So I went to get my car keys and start heading through the door. I guess getting my car keys and motioning to leave without saying so much as goodbye was a big deal for him, because everything that followed happened very quickly.

He grabbed me by the sides of my shirt with such force that he spun me around. My blouse twisted around my waist and I ended up right in front of him. My eyes opened wide with terror because it was such an unexpected reaction to such a simple statement. Alex was getting ready in her room so she didn't hear the commotion. And, as usual, the TV in the family room was blaring.

"What did you just say?" he asked.

"I w-w-w-want to go to the s-s-store with our d-d-d-daughter," I stammered.

"Who told you that you are free enough to do that?" His blood was boiling.

"No one."

"No one? What does that mean? Answer me. Who *told* you that you are free enough to do that? Did I not tell you that *I* am your god? You are not free to go anywhere unless I tell you to go?"

I didn't answer.

"Did I not tell you that you don't go anywhere without me? Give me the keys," he commanded.

I held fast to them.

"Drop your purse."

I held on tighter than I had before.

He grabbed my purse from me and threw it into the laundry room. The zipper burst and everything in it came gushing out everywhere. I felt as though he had just burst me open. Then he took my keys and threw them in my face. I tried to duck so they wouldn't gouge my eyes out, but I wasn't fast enough because I felt the stinging of the keys piercing the skin on the side of my face before I knew what was happening.

He, next, put his palm to my forehead and shoved me into the couch. "Please, stop! The neighbors can hear!" I still had the sliding glass doors open.

"*That's* what I'm talking about. *You* are the reason why nobody respects me around here. *You* are the one who told lies on me and people won't talk to me. If I could hit you, I would tear your face up and beat you so bad that you'd be bloody and black and blue."

Out of the corner of my eye, I saw a movement. I saw Alex walk from her bedroom.

She was standing at the entrance to the family room. *Oh my goodness I thought, she gets to witness her father's cruelty towards me.*

"Daddy, what are you doing?" she timidly asked.

"Get out of here!" he shouted at her.

"I'm not leaving," came her calculated response.

"See what you've done?" he said turning back to me. "You've turned my child against me. You know how you've turned her against me! She doesn't listen to me. Now I can't tell her anything!"

"Please –" I began.

"SHUT YOUR F----- MOUTH!" he suddenly exploded. "Didn't I tell you to shut the f--- up? What the f-- did I tell you? I said you are NOBODY! SHUT UP!" I wasn't talking at this point.

"Please –" I began.

"I SAID SHUT THE F--- UP! I have a good feeling to just *beat* you against this wall until you're black and blue! WHO TOLD YOU THAT YOU COULD LEAVE HERE? WHO TOLD YOU THAT YOU WERE ALLOWED TO TAKE MY CHILD AND GO SOMEWHERE? WITHOUT *ME*?"

I was sitting there as calm and as still as a stone. I did not know what I was supposed to do, because I feared if I so much as blinked, he would kill me. I didn't know what he was going to do next. All I could do was pray *God, help me.* I must have not realized it, but I said that out loud instead of keeping it inside my head.

"*God help you?*" he repeated. "Didn't I *tell* you that *I* am your god? Didn't I tell you *I* am the one you bow down to? Who *told* you otherwise?"

I finally got smart and decided to just keep my mouth shut. My daughter, with all the bravery that a seven-year old could muster in a situation like this, came and sat beside me. The next words out of her mouth stunned my heart into almost stopping completely.

"Daddy, please stop."

"Really?" he taunted, his voice taking on new dimensions. Then he went over to the kitchen counter and brought back a knife.

I saw my life flash before my eyes. I saw the funeral casket they would use for me, and the white one they would probably use for my baby girl, just to prove how much more innocent she was. I saw my mother hysterical and beside herself, weeping cries of deep sorrow over the lost lives of her daughter *and* her granddaughter. And I saw *him* standing over our grave, tilting his head back and cackling like Satan over the victory he had won.

"Let me tell you something," he said, while carelessly waving the knife before both of our faces. "I can cut you up right now and you would just *disappear*. And you know what they would do to me? They would just take me to jail and lock me up. And I would just tell them I was insane. And what would they do with me? They would just lock me up in a cell for the rest of my life. And I would just sit in that cell and not do anything much different than what I do here every day. I'd just watch TV all day long. And where would you be, bitch, hmm? You would be in your grave and nothing else would come out of your life. Nobody else would ever see your ugly face again. Nobody else would hear from you again. And that meaningless, dumb dream you have of one day getting out of this will *never* come true. Because *I* am your god and *I* am in control."

I sat there, barely able to take a breath, daring myself not to breathe, because I couldn't believe what was happening. He might as well have taken the knife and jabbed it into my lungs because the wind had been completely knocked out of me. I gave his words some thought: *Is this really all that would come out of my life? And what about the innocent child I brought into this world? Her only purpose was to just be killed by her own malevolent father?*

As I was sitting there, motionless and lost in thought, I felt a sensation close to my ribs. It was the knife.

"I could slice you right here. And if I cut you right now, I would take *her* out too," he said, motioning to our daughter. "And *nothing*, absolutely *nothing* would come out of your miserable life. You're nothing but a *stinking mess of flesh*. I could make you disappear and nobody would even remember that you were ever here."

I couldn't stare at him because if I looked at him, I believe he would have *hurt* me in unthinkable ways. I stared straight ahead at the TV and I didn't dare breathe. It felt like I was waiting. Waiting on him to either put the knife down and pretend like this never happened, or waiting on him to do just as he said he would and do away with both my precious daughter and me in a few swift movements.

Then it started to happen in slow motion. I watched the knife get closer to my body, and I felt it edging closer and closer to my flesh. *Surely*, I thought, *there must be a God in Heaven.*

In the silence preceding this slow motion sequence, I heard my daughter's angelic voice in her fortitude and fearlessness say something.

"Daddy, please don't hurt me and Mommy."

Something broke in him. The fire burning in his eyes retracted, the quivering muscles ceased, and finally, his face fell. Whatever murderous demon possessed him left without so much as a huff. He must have come back to his right mind (if he really ever had one).

He looked down at the knife, and then he looked at the two of us sitting there on the couch. The next sound I heard was a clattering muffled thud of the knife as he dropped the knife on the kitchen counter.

"Oh my God," he said, the ramifications of what he was about to do apparent in his voice, and his face.

"Oh my God," he repeated. *Oh my God indeed*.

"I'm so sorry," he said, and he tried to hug my little angel, but she was crying, and she forcefully resisted his attempts at embracing her.

"Baby," he said, true sorrow in his voice, "I'm so sorry. *Please* forgive Daddy. *Please* don't try to ever remember this."

Tearfully, she said, "Daddy, how could you want to hurt me and Mommy? You could have *killed* my Mommy!" She almost yelled that part.

"Honey, I'm *sorry*. I don't know what happened to me; I don't know what came over me.

But I'm going to ask you and your Mommy to *please* forgive me. *Please*…"

Then, just like that, he walked away.

And then, just like that, it was over.

After what felt like an eternity of gathering my bearings together and comforting my daughter (as well as thanking God for the life I still had), I got up.

I walked over to the counter, picked up my keys, got my daughter, and went to the store.

A few days later, he said, "It's time for us to move. Too many bad things have happened to us in this neighborhood and in this house. I'd like you to look around for a house, somewhere closer to the city so you don't have to feel so far away from your friends. I know you like to meet with your friends. I'll do whatever you say; whatever you'll ask, I'll do; and whatever you agree to is what I will agree to."

I was used to his ever-changing nature by now. One minute, he's Lucifer reincarnate. The very next second, he's your best friend, your most loyal confidante, and your most faithful friend. His shifts in mood were worse than those in any person who suffered from even the most severe form of Schizophrenia. It was clear that it was time for a fresh start.

The fresh start began when we moved into a beautiful, nicely appointed home in a suburb closer to the city. It was much bigger than the previous house we lived in and the neighborhood was far more developed than the previous neighborhood. The previous occupants of the home were very kind to us; they were moving into a newly built home and were quick to make sure we were safely moved into their old home.

We started to make friends with the people on the block. One particular neighbor, who lived three houses down from us, was a grandmother raising her two granddaughters by herself. The granddaughters, who were around my daughter's age, quickly befriended my daughter and the three of them struck up an attachment to one another. They all went to the same school and rode on the same school bus. Life settled down calmly in that quiet little alcove of a neighborhood.

Sam became more isolated as my daughter and I socialized more. Whereas he had been the one to encourage me to move, he turned the accusations around and began accusing *me* of being the cause of us moving. He now claimed that nothing was wrong with the house we left and we were better off staying there (even though he had despised the neighbors there because he felt they all 'turned' against him). He even went as far as saying that we moved away from all of his friends. *What friends?* He didn't have any friends in the suburb we lived in before; all of his friends were in the city. And since we now lived closer to the city, I thought he would have been more grateful than he was acting. But my expectations were far too great.

Then he began his usual pattern of isolating me from as many people as possible. I still had my job at the call center. Now that we moved, I was farther away from it. That was a delight to me, but a personal offense to him. I learned later that he used to drive around the parking lot looking for my car to see if I were really there or not.

In this neighborhood, the houses were closer together. You could literally hear your neighbor without having to raise your voice. While my voice was low and timid most of the time and the neighbors couldn't hear me, he made *certain* the neighbors heard him. As I started moving around in the community, I started going to a local hairdresser who befriended me. One day, I was at the salon getting my hair done when one of her friends who introduced herself as Julie, a Sales Director of a large cosmetics company, spotted me. She asked me if I would be interested in selling cosmetics as a sales representative. It would help me make some extra cash on the side.

I decided to do it because I figured I wouldn't have anything to lose. When she signed me up, of course *he* disagreed with it under the 'they just rip you off and take your money' guise. Anything that would bring me closer to achieving complete financial freedom from him was something he violently opposed.

One day, Julie called and she offered me an opportunity to model cosmetics and dresses for a fashion show she was having. I agreed to participate and made arrangements to go to the show. Of course, *he* didn't like it one bit.

I think Julie suspected I was being abused and gently suggested that the fashion show was targeted at a female audience so as to discourage him from coming. This, however, didn't work. He insisted on coming, even though he really didn't have to come. Julie and her assistant, Sarah, had always invited me to events to model and sell cosmetics, but I never got to go to them.

They finally asked me why I was never in attendance to these events. I told them that my husband never let me come to these events and whenever I did, it was a 'problem'. I then finally broke down and told them he was abusive. I couldn't admit he actually hit me (I hadn't reached that level of emotional healing just yet), but I just used the word 'abuse' ambiguously without giving any specific definition.

Julie invited me to attend a casual dinner and fashion show she was hosting. Little did I know that it was just a ruse to introduce me to her husband, who was a deputy sheriff. I knew right then and there that Sam would be opposed to it. Still I tried asking him. I told him in order to make it to the fashion show on time, I wouldn't be able to leave work and come home to get ready; he would have to drive from home and meet me there.

He didn't like that because that meant my every waking minute wouldn't be accounted for. Any situation that removed the element of control from him was something he violently opposed. He, instead, wanted me to leave work and then come to pick him up from home to drive him back to the event. It didn't make any sense time-wise, but *he* was never one to make sense. When I told him I was going to the event from work as it made more sense time-wise, he threatened that I would have a problem when I came home. I went anyway.

I was surprised at how much fun I had. I modeled, laughed, socialized with women my own age, ate, and just had a very good, wholesome evening. When Julie Introduced me to her husband, it was as if he already knew more about me than I did about myself.

"I understand you're married?" he asked. I nodded. He then gave me his card (with his official title on it) and told me if I ever had a problem that I should give him a call.

I knew that my time at the fashion show was limited because I had been forewarned by *him* to make sure I got home by a certain time and to call him every hour. As soon as the show was over, I apologized profusely for having to leave quickly and rushed out to get home by my 'curfew'. I knew that socializing after events like these were customary, but I had a pre-determined schedule. In the mad dash to get home, the meeting with the Sheriff flew out of my mind and I forgot about it.

While driving, I called Sam on my cell phone to let him know I was on my way. As soon as he answered, he said, "Just because you have a cell phone now and you feel you can drive wherever you want doesn't mean that you're more important than I am."

"It's not about that. It's never been about that. Can we just please not argue tonight?"

He mumbled rather unintelligibly. When he was done, I asked him if I could speak to Alex and he said no. He wouldn't even let her come near the phone even though I could hear her in the background asking to speak to me. Then, he hung up. I called back, however the phone rang without answer. Unknown to me, he had pulled the phone jack out of the wall.

When I finally got home, would you believe he had his car parked horizontally across the driveway blocking my car from getting into the garage? Here I was sitting in my car after a long day, trying to come home and see my daughter, trying to come home to get some rest from having to work long hours seven days a week, and here was this two-faced man preventing me from entering my own home. I couldn't go to a motel and stay for the night because I had no money; paying the mortgage and the bills on our new house absorbed my most recent paycheck.

As I sat there with nothing to do, he sat there in his car, yelling and taunting me.

"I'm not letting you in my f---- house because I want the neighbors to know what a bitch you are because all you do is go out and whore all around the damn place!" he shouted across the street so everyone could hear. You have to understand it was late at night and everyone was in his or her home and within earshot of what he was saying.

Whore around? I thought. *Where would I find time to go whore around when I was working seven days a week at 14 hours per day to pay all of his bills? When did I find time to be a whore?*

I didn't say anything. I just sat in the car, waiting for this tyrannical phase of his to end so I could wipe my makeup off and go to my bed. I noticed the street was strangely quiet. All the lights in the homes were off, and there was not so much as a dog's bark coming from anyone's back yard.

I realized then the neighbors were listening and watching what was going on. In an attempt to make me think they weren't doing so, they turned off the lights and TVs in their homes and shushed all their pets to make it seem like they were asleep. It was also then I realized at the slightest sign of trouble, they had every intention to call the police. They were tired of hearing him yell at me and they decided they were going to do something about it.

As I sat in the car, I thought *what do I do?* My answer came in the form of my almost eight-year old daughter.

With all of her fearlessness, she decided that she had enough of her father's shenanigans. She walked through the front door, walked around his car, and made her way to my car, which was parked on the curb near the mailbox.

He was so shocked at her gusto that he was rendered speechless for a moment.

"What are you doing out here sweetie? Go back inside the house," he said.

"No, I'm not going back inside the house," she snapped at him in a daring tone. "I want my mommy to come inside."

And he had the audacity to tell her "No, your mommy can't come in because she's a whoring bitch who went out all evening to her fancy cocktail party without me and she thinks she's better than me."

Alex didn't say one word; she just stood there and stared him down. Then she spoke.

"Daddy, I'm going to tell you this for the last time. If you do not move your car and let my mother drive in, I am going to scream so loud that the neighbors will call the police. And when the police come, I'm going to tell them *exactly* what you have been doing to my mommy. Now *do you hear me?*" Even she intimidated me at this point.

I have never seen *him* move so fast. He got in that car and parked it in the garage so quickly that one would have never known the same man who had just been threatening me gave in to an eight year old girl's demands.

When my daughter had finished making her pronouncement, while he was parking the car properly, she walked down to my car and got in. She said, "Mommy, you can drive in now." And she sat with me in the car until I drove safely into the garage.

She was just like my private guardian angel, watching over me dutifully and protecting me from the evils of my husband. As I shut the garage door down, my heart was thudding so violently. I thought that as soon I walked in through the garage door, I was dead.

But when I opened the door to get in, Alex was standing right beside me. She asked me if I was hungry and I said no; I was too terrified to feel anything but fear. I probably was hungry, but the panic I felt drove out any natural human feelings.

"If you're not going to eat, then I will stay with you while you wipe your makeup off and have a bath, and I will sleep in your room tonight." Then she turned to her father and said, "Now look. I have to go to bed because I want to sleep tonight because I have a test in school tomorrow. *You're* going to sit out here, daddy, and you're going to sleep in the family room and you're *not* going to disturb my mommy or me. Now go to bed and good night!"

And she turned around, pushed me into the bedroom and stayed with me until it was time for me to go to bed. In this new house, the master bedroom was large enough to accommodate a loveseat. Alex got comfortable for the night.

"Mommy he's not going to come in here to hurt or bother you. Trust me; he won't."

As I lay in bed that night, I thought *this couldn't continue to go on. I cannot place my eight-year-old child in such danger. This is too emotionally traumatic for her.* She had to always be on the defense. How was I sure he wouldn't one day turn on her the way he had turned on me?

Furthermore, statistics showed the older a child gets in domestic violence situations, the more likely the abuser will turn his attention to the child. This *has* to end.

I realistically took a look at my situation. I didn't have a green card; I didn't really have that much money. But I knew that I *had* to find a way to get out of it.

Because of the shame and the humiliation the abuse had caused, I was unable to voice my feelings. I never told *anyone* what was going on. I *never* told anyone about the abuse, or the hell, or anything that was going on.

I think I wanted someone to help me, but for some reason, the abuse was never shown to others. I always did a great job of hiding bruises, cuts and scars. But, nonetheless, I never told a soul what I was going through. It was later on I realized I should have spoken up because no one was going to speak up for me.

I figured there had to be a way to get help. *I don't know how, I don't know when, but I have to find it some way.*

After that night, the situation in the home quickly deteriorated. I was trapped in a fiery furnace and a very violent marriage. The marriage wasn't defined by the vows we had taken; it was, instead, defined by what *he* dictated it should be defined by. I had completely run out of options.

I used to be able to leave early in the morning and go to work to escape from him; that ended when he started checking my hours. The only days I had off were Sundays. I would stay up into the late hours of the night cleaning the house and doing everything in my power to not go into the bedroom. Our marriage wasn't one that had any physical intimacy.

Getting up to go to church was a fight. As soon as church was over, I would come home, fix dinner, and then take a nap. For whatever reason, he never bothered me on Sunday afternoons. As the evening wore on, the abuse would start. I could time him; at exactly six o'clock every Sunday evening, he would start.

The abuse had finally begun to take its wear on my physical and mental capacities. All the energy I entered into the marriage with was beginning to drain from me, and with no sign of escape, I began to lose hope.

9
Keys

One morning, he tricked me. By this time, Alex was being picked up by the school bus. I would normally shower before he left to take his 'morning drive' so that by the time he got back, I was out the door and on my way to work. But this morning, I had decided to stall before I bathed. And I had even decided to have a bath instead of a shower.

It was an ordinary spring day. I thought I would have at least half an hour or about 45 minutes to get dressed before he returned. As soon as I stepped out of the bath, he was standing in the bathroom doorway.

His presence felt more like an invader in the house than anything else. There I was just coming out of the bathtub, naked, confused and scared.

He started walking towards me and the realization of what was about to happen dawned on me. *Oh my God. Please let it be quick, Lord.*

I thought about trying to run and I realized there was nowhere to run. I couldn't climb through the window, nor could I make a dash for the bedroom because he was blocking my only exit.

"How long do you expect me to live like this?" he asked. "You haven't had sex with me. You give your body to every man who looks at you. What are you going to do now? You treat me like I'm your brother. I'm not your brother. I'm a man and I'm your husband. You're supposed to give me what I bought when I married you."

All kinds of thoughts were running through my head. *What the hell does he mean he bought me? He hasn't bought one damn thing since this marriage began.*

"Come here!" he yelled.

I was startled.

"Come where? I'm right here." I knew that trying to distract him wasn't going to work; I gave it a shot anyway.

"I called you, woman. *Come here!*"

I was naked in the physical form, and I felt emotionally naked. He had already stripped down my confidence, my dignity, and my sanity. Now he was going to strip away from me the one thing I had left that I could call my own? I was trapped, and it finally dawned on me that I spent most of this marriage being trapped. The voice in my head screamed it was time to get out of this trap called a marriage. But that time was not now.

I didn't know when he got close enough to grab me because I don't remember him advancing towards me suddenly. My legs felt like liquid as they gave out from under me. The last time he attacked me like this, he had a knife. I had no clue what other instrument of death he would choose this time.

It was until he shoved me on the bed and pinned himself on top of me that I realized there was no point in going to a spiritual hell, because I was already living one, here in the earthly realm.

He *forced* himself in me so hard it felt like I would get, among other things, rug burn. And, despite my cries and whimpers for him to do the contrary, he raped me.

My entire body went into paralytic shock as I gasped at the sheer physical anguish this was causing me. My body tightening up only increased the suffering and increased the pleasure on his. It felt as though he were trying with all his might to carve out a hole in my body, a hole that would be left gaping open.

It didn't matter that he had already emotionally and verbally raped me. It didn't matter that he had already physically beat me within an inch of my life. What mattered was he was taking something that was supposed to remain intimate and, instead, using it to violate and punish me for some unthinkable crime. My body shuddered with disgust, disgust at him for being who he was, and disgust at myself for allowing him to be who he was. In those few moments I wanted nothing more than to die.

To add insult to injury, he kept repeating over and over again *you're my wife; you* give *this to me; you're not supposed to withhold anything from me; how* dare *you keep yourself from me; you're nothing but a worthless whore…* throughout the humiliating process, over and over and over and over and over and over again.

When *he* saw it fit to finish, he got up, zipped up his pants and walked away. All I could do was kneel on the side of the bed and whimper. I was too weak to scream, to bawl, and to even die. I felt just so hopeless, and so bare. *Nothing* in his pattern of abuse had prepared me for that.

It was the ringing of the telephone that interrupted my desolate thoughts. The rings of the phone sounded more like the driving of nails into my coffin. All he did was get up and leave me in a broken heap, raped and ridded of any trace of dignity I had left. What a mess I had found myself in. *How do I get out of this?*

There is a song that says *'Let the weak say I am strong'.* I tried as hard as I could to find my strength in those after-moments. But I couldn't. I had no strength left. I had *nothing* left. Somehow, some way, I *had* to get out of this. Somehow, moving into that cursed house was going to present me with the keys to my freedom. It was just a matter of finding them.

10
Away

From that point on, I called the rape an incident because I didn't want to acknowledge the fact that I had truly become a victim of rape. The media did not paint a pleasant picture of women who suffered domestic violence; they were often depicted as women who had been left behind by men and lived lives filled with much poverty and shame. Nothing in my upbringing groomed or prepared me to live such a life, so I chose to purposefully not acknowledge or admit what was going on.

I was no longer in control of the situation (not that I ever really was) because I was now the dictionary definition of victim. A man who had purported to be a husband and father to our child had victimized me. Whether I liked it or not, my circumstances had now placed me in the category of *helpless*. I had become hostage to an individual who now held the reigns of my life. And my life had shifted into overdrive far sooner than I wanted. There was nothing I could do to contain or control the events around me.

My coping mechanisms were, at best, minimal. I now had nothing else with which to cope. I had become worn down from the physical battering and emotional abuse. These afflictions had now been compounded by rape; the pain was unbearable. *To whom could I turn?*

For days, I drove around mindlessly. I would leave early to go to work and find myself in parking lots at malls; I would park the car and keep the air conditioner running, just sitting there. Sometimes I would fall asleep because that was the only place I could find peace to sleep. I'd find myself walking around shopping malls looking at other mothers who had their children with them, seemingly enjoying the bright, sunny days and a chance to shop.

That's all I ever wanted - to have a casual outing with my own daughter. I wanted to spend bonding time with her to remind her how normal life could be.

My shifts at work normalized, so now instead of leaving work at 9 pm, I could now leave at 6 pm. For anyone else, those were normal hours. But nothing in my life was normal. I would find myself at shopping malls waiting for the darkness to come before I left for home; waiting for night to fall because I couldn't contend with the emotional, physical and verbal abuse.

Many nights before I went home, I would send up a prayer that by the time I got home, peace would be there waiting on me; peace to replace the violent, tumultuous atmosphere. Sometimes I felt like my existence was pointless. After all, what's the purpose of coming into this world only to be treated as my *being* was futile?

At work, the effects of the abuse were beginning to take their toll on my encounters with co-workers. I became sensitive and would cry if someone raised his or her voice at me. Because I worked at a call center, I talked to people who had problems with their cell phones all day long. If someone became even slightly loud, or raised their voice a smidgen, I would start to cry. I remember my supervisor removing me from the phones one time because I broke down in tears. The reason? A man raised his voice at me on the phone. I became overly sensitive; what people said around me heightened my emotions.

One day at work, there was a guy who took a liking to me. Unfortunately for him, he was tall and dark, just like *Sam*. As he started walking towards me in the parking lot, I started to back towards the car. He said that he wasn't trying to hurt me; he just wanted to say hello and ask me out. I was so terrified that I flew into the car and locked all my doors before he had a chance to say anything else.

He reported the incident to one of my supervisors because he thought that *I* would file a complaint. When I walked into work the next day, Cindy asked to see me.

"Is everything ok?" she asked when I walked into her office.

"Yes, of course. Why?" I had learned how to become a master liar at this point.

"Well, Tom just said he saw you in the parking lot and you seemed to have been apprehensive of him to the point where he's worried. Are you *sure* everything's ok?"

"That was nothing," I said, attempting to laugh it off. The laugh came out as more of a choke. "I was just startled, that's all."

"I want you to know that anything you tell me will be in the strictest confidence."

"Ok. That's good and all, but I have nothing to tell."

She still didn't give up. "I want you to know that if there's *anything* you need help with, you can come to me and ask me for help. We're here for you, ok?"

"Ok, but, there's nothing to tell," I repeated. Then it was over and I went back to work.

Little did I know I was really going to need her help later on. I pushed the 'incident' to the back of my mind and left it there. In the meantime,

I struggled to find a way to break through the pattern of abuse, a way to ratify my circumstances to bring about some normalcy to my life. I had a daughter for whom I had sole responsibility because her father was incapable of handling his financial and emotional responsibilities.

It was left up to me to find a way to bring about some sort of planning and certainty to her future. It was more than obvious we could not continue to live in our environment. At some point, just as it had wreaked havoc on me, it was bound to wreak emotional havoc on her. It was left up to me to find a solution. One way or another, this marriage had to be dissolved. It was either that or I faced the grim prospect of being sent to a grave by my husband.

So I decided to look around for help. As I began to look around for what resources existed in the community, I came across a young lady with whom I became friendly (she happened to be my hairstylist). I had finally come to the realization that I should confide in someone. I told her about emotional and verbal abuse, and, to a very slight extent, the physical abuse. But, I didn't tell her everything because I feared her reaction.

I was ashamed of the pain stemming from the abuse. The shame of the events that occurred was so debilitating it forced me into silence, silence about the turmoil I was enduring at home. I felt broken and violated because I had been treated so badly by a man I was intimate with and whom I had married.

I felt let down and abandoned. I had given myself to him and shared the most private parts of my being with him. For him to turn around and throw it back in my face, by raping me and treating me as though I were less than nothing, was something my mind had a hard time grasping.

Many times I thought I had lost my mind. In an effort to deal and cope with it, I clinically detached myself from it. I spoke of it as though it happened to someone else, but not to me. I couldn't personalize it. Because I couldn't personalize it, I couldn't talk about it. I couldn't express to someone else what was happening without making it seem as though it were just a one-time occurrence. The emotional damage it did over time was such that it wore me down. If I faced it, then I would have had serious problems in dealing with myself. I would not have been able to survive or come through it.

I dealt with it by being as emotionally removed from it as I possibly could. Somehow I was still able to confide in this woman. Her recommendation was to at least start by going to the pastor of the church I attended for counseling. I called the church office and requested a meeting with the pastor to have counseling. The permission was granted. Of course, *Sam* had no idea what I was doing.

By this time, the year 2000 had come. While there was newness to the millennium, there was no newness to my situation. It seemed to be the continuing melodrama. It seemed to be one continuous, horrid, lifetime experience that was relentless in the emotional havoc it wreaked on my life. And it seemed as though this situation was barreling down a one-way street to my destruction.

I went to see the Pastor. I had every hope that he was somehow going to give me some sort of spiritual epiphany. He listened to my story and asked me my husband's ethnicity. I told him and he said it seemed like men of that ethnicity seem to be controlling.

"You're not the first woman in the church of your background who has come forward to admit that. Here's what *has* to happen: you *have* to get out of this marriage. You *cannot* continue to live in this situation. You *must* get out. And as much I hate to be the one to tell you this, your marriage is over. It's time for you to go. You *have* to do so *as quickly as possible*. There is no use trying to hang on. There's *nothing* left. You *must* get away."

As I sat in his office, I realized the words he had just spoken were like the reading of my sentence. They were simply confirmation of what I had already perceived to be the truth. But to hear someone else mouth it and put it into words was more than enough to convince me of the situation's nature. As tears streamed down my face, he consoled me.

"But it's going to be alright. There is life after divorce. I, myself, am a survivor of divorce. And I'm now happier than I've ever been. So you, too, will find happiness. My prayer for you is you will experience joy a loving marriage can bring. But it is important now you get out of this marriage. No good thing will come out of it."

As I stood to walk out of his office, I knew it was really over. I turned back to look at him, realizing he had just spoken the right words to give me courage I needed to face what was in front of me. The question burning in my mind was *how is this going to happen?*

I *so* did not want a confrontation because that would mean physical violence. If I had to encounter any more physical violence, I would suffer a catastrophic breakdown. All previous physical confrontations ran through my mind, and they all seemed to have one thing in common: me being beaten. I didn't know what on earth I would do. *He* had a penchant for hitting me in what he would call the 'soft places', where no one could see the bruises, but I could feel them and they hurt like hell. There's nothing like a fist sucker punched right into your stomach that draws the very life and breath out of you. But there are some things that can't be avoided.

When you live with an abusive, controlling person, there is no such thing as peace and quiet. They set the tone for everything in the home and the tone typically set is one of violence, anger, frustration, rage, and misery.

I got in my car and drove out of the church parking lot. As I drove, I wished there was some magic way to make this all disappear. I wished there was some way to make everything just go *away*. I wished I could walk away from this marriage as easily as I had just walked out of the pastor's office. I even envied him and the peace he had. He seemed to have a certain joy and I wondered if I had been cheated out of that. I used to look at other people who were married and who appeared to be happy together. I used to wonder if that really existed or if it was all a façade, a masquerade they were putting on because that same happiness didn't apply to me.

As I drove away that morning, I knew I had to face the un-faceable. I knew I had to find a way to make this work. There had to be a way for me to get out of the marriage with my life, my mind, my emotions, and, most importantly, my daughter intact. Even if it meant I had to walk away from the house and the lifestyle, I *had* to get away.

But how is this going to be possible? Where am I going to live? How am I going to get from one place to the other? The answer would come while at my job, little did I know.

As I was driving, I let my imagination wonder. *Let me imagine what kind of life I will have if I get out of this*, I thought. It seemed idyllic to just *imagine* how free I could be to go to work, to get in my car and drive anywhere I wanted to at any time I wanted to, and be free to make my own decisions, even free to sleep.

I imagined a home with no quarreling, no abuse, no shouting, no yelling, no pushing, and no shoving. Believe me when I tell you I would have given *anything* to go home one evening and not have someone meet me at the door to shove me into the wall; not have someone push me into a couch; not have someone slap me across my face; not have someone to threaten to kick me out of my own house; not have someone lift their foot up at me and kick me to the door. I wondered what it would feel like. The freedom I so desperately craved and envied was just a few months away.

When I got to work that day, I was feeling a thousand times better. I literally bounced into the office. I sat down in the break room and opened my lunch container. The cover of the container made a distinct popping noise as I lifted it from the container. The sound in the silent, empty break room startled me. The sound of the lid popping off the container sounded like a lid popping off my life. *That* was the sound of freedom, of *my* freedom.

As the turntable in the microwave spun around and around, all I could see was the turmoil and the events in my marriage mimicking the turntable; round and round and round it went. When the microwave beeped indicating that the time was up and done, I thought the beeping was expressive of my marriage now being up and done. As I sat at the table and lifted the fork to my mouth, I recalled sitting at a table and first meeting *Sam*. My memory took me to the very first time I sat across a table from *him* to have dinner. I saw myself being full of hope and feeling light and in love. I saw us living in the first house we shared; I saw all the people we had known and had been friends with over the years; I saw myself getting married and the frown looking back at me in the looking glass.

I remembered the certainty in my heart telling me I shouldn't get married; I remembered my best friend, at the time, who promised if I married him, I would never see her again (and I never did); I remembered us packing up and moving; I remembered the sounds of the all the people and events making up my life to that point. It all flashed by before my eyes.

I've never mentioned how very fond Sam was of the colors black, white, and red. The perfect design for him was always a red background with black and white accessories. I *hated* that. To me, it seemed like he always preferred colors of mourning and death. To this day, I don't wear red often and I strongly dislike the color because it had been so much a part of my abusive marriage. I saw the black and white plates he loved and prized. And I saw myself taking those plates and shattering them on the ground to millions of little pieces. I knew the end had come. I didn't know how much longer there was; I did know within a few short months, a marriage would be over. *Finally*, I thought happily. *I can't wait*.

Here I was on a random Thursday morning, sitting in a break room in an office complex finally realizing after 13 years, this blood-filled, loveless marriage was coming to a screeching halt. All of the control *he* had insisted on implementing and using against me had no power to hold me because I was now going to be free. I realized the freedom came from within my mind. The ability to be free had always existed. But because I never experienced it before, I didn't know I could ever live it.

To all the persons who are reading this book, I admonish you, if you're going through *anything*, you *must* speak up. Don't do as I did and keep it to yourself and silently scream, hoping someone will hear you and come to your rescue; only *you* can come to your rescue. I can say this with confidence because the moment I chose to speak up, someone pointed me in the right direction. That person started unlocking the door, which kept me bound to a life that condemned me to a life of poverty and destruction designed to kill me. This was not poverty in the financial sense; this was poverty from lack of hope. Now, here I was, being given the keys to freedom. It's not enough to go through abuse and not say anything. You've *got* to speak up.

I knew the perfect opportunity to get out of it and be free forever was going to present itself. All I had to do was to have patience and wait. *What more do I have to lose?*

I had been waiting for that day for so long. I lived in the greatest country on earth, the country that recognizes freedom of the individual. *I, too, shall be free.*

I got up from the table and went back to my desk with a smile on my face.

11
Release

He had a penchant for using money as part of his system of control. When we sold the previous house we lived in, we made a tidy little profit. The agreement we had was we would put the money away for Alex's college fund. But *Sam* had other plans. Oh Sam, what more could you want, haven't I given enough already? But Sam couldn't have enough. Enough was never enough.

Sam came to me with some story that he wanted to go to replace his Rolex watch collection he had lost. I thought it was an unreasonable thing to ask.

"Rolex watches? In place of Alex's college fund? You would *really* be so selfish that you would spend so much money on buying some watches when you could have put money away for her college fund?"

Right then and there, he slapped me across my face.

"How many times have I told you not to question me? It's *my* f--- money and I can do whatever the heck I want with it, bitch! Don't you *ever* ask me about it again. Now, I want you to go to the bank, get my bleeping money, and bring my f---- money to me. And don't ask me another question."

Because of his mounting tax troubles with the IRS, he could not keep money in his name. This was something he neglected to tell me about when we got married. Had he told me this; I would have never entered into any kind of financial obligation with him.

I had no idea of his tax troubles until we filed a tax return and received a letter from the IRS in which they told me point-blank I was getting no returns because *he* owed money to them. He felt the government was investigating him. As part of this ruse, he claimed he couldn't keep money in his name. This is why he always kept money in *my* name (even though I was not allowed to use it).

I decided the money we had in the bank was all we had left. It wasn't considered much at the time, only $25,000. I was clinging to it in the hopes if I ever got my freedom, it would be somewhere for me to start. I had some money put away in stocks for my daughter's college fund. I felt confident enough the money would have given my daughter and I a way to start over.

I refused to give him the money. But he insisted, and I caved because I didn't know what else to do. He had already blocked me from entering the house, beaten me, slapped me like he was my pimp and I his whore, had already threatened to kill me numerous times, and had even threatened to come to my job and haul me away kicking and screaming; he preyed on my fear of embarrassment. He insisted that he needed $15,000. So I withdrew that amount in cashier's check and gave it to him.

That weekend he took off on a visit to see his friends in Miami. I thought he, knowing the marriage was coming to an end, was buying property to retire after it was over. I had no interest in his future plans. I was just thankful my daughter and I had two days to us while he disappeared. Those two days of peace felt like two years of bliss. I didn't even go to work because I earned the right to call in sick. So I stayed at home and slept and pretended I was living a normal life.

In the meantime, I had developed a friendship with the neighbor down the street. I used to go to her house and talk to her. She took a liking to me because her daughter, who was around my age, had moved away. She used to ask me where my mother and other family members were and I told her how far away they lived. She used to fix things for us, like muffins and cakes. Sometimes she would let my daughter come off the school bus and stay at her house for a little while before coming home. And she would have enough courage to stand up to *him* whenever he questioned her. She knew what she was doing; she was giving my little angel just enough freedom from her father to feel like a normal kid.

One day, my neighbor's daughter came to visit and I met her. She was such a sweetheart; she said her mother had told her all about me and she hoped things would one day work out. I was near to tears (in those days, I was very sensitive; if a fly flew across my path, I would cry). I couldn't stand kindness when it was given to me because so much of my daily existence was lived in an atmosphere of extreme emotional depravity, and the man I married had been as mean and cruel to me as possible.

I couldn't grasp when someone would say something nice to me because it was a gesture I had never had pleasure of experiencing.

If the people who live in your house with you don't like you, then, after a while, you begin to think there must be something seriously wrong with you. Sometimes, total strangers would tell me I was a nice and great person, and it would throw me off.

While *he* was out of town, I took the opportunity to explore options to get me closer to freedom. I started to do some research on the Internet. My daughter had become an expert at surfing the Internet and finding resources through the Internet. One evening, she had a surprise waiting for me. She went on the Internet and found the perfect house for she and I to live in one day. She made it sound so simple: "We could move in and daddy wouldn't even know, mommy!" She even went as far as doing a virtual tour of the house. I laughed at her naïveté because I knew that it wasn't so simple. Since my income was already tied up in paying one mortgage, I doubted anyone would have approved me for a second one. But it was still encouraging to know Alex was optimistic our lives would one day become normal.

I had borrowed some money from a finance company to pay down on my first car. I had since traded that car in and bought a newer, better car. I had paid off the loan before the deadline was up. When I went to make the final payment, Kathy at the finance company took one look at me and said, "You're in trouble, aren't you?"

Baffled, I asked "What trouble?"

"Ma'am, you've been coming in here for twelve months; I know abuse when I see it." Her ability to pinpoint my situation with such ease shocked me. "Sit down," she gently commanded.

"What I'm about to tell you is going to help you. Your marriage is over."

I thought to myself *this whole 'your marriage is over' thing must be going around. Has she spoken to my pastor? This is the second person telling me this in the space of two weeks.*

"The man you are married to is the kind of man who will not pay alimony or child support. In fact, he will make sure you walk out of that marriage *penniless*. If he hasn't done so already, he has taken all the money out of the joint account, unknown to you. He's been taking money out and telling you he's buying things when this is far from the truth. The only thing you have left is the house. He's not going to continue to help pay the mortgage. When you leave, he's going to default on the mortgage, just to ensure that you won't have a house. Here is my suggestion. Does he have credit card debt?"

Stupefied, I said, "Yes."

"Do you have credit card debt?"

"Yes."

"I want you to go home, write out how much you owe to the credit card companies and bring a copy of your mortgage statement so I can see how much you owe on the mortgage. Based on your previous loan history with us, we can take over that mortgage, pay off your credit card debt, and pay off your car. It's called a debt consolidation. We'll consolidate all your debt and you just pay one monthly payment. That means you'll get the title to your car for free and you will have your car free and clear. That's the only thing you're going to get out of this marriage. Believe me you're going to need your car to go to work to pay the mounting lawyer's fees."

"Oh my God," I said, "That actually sounds like it might work. But how am I going to convince him? There's no way he's going to want to do it."

"What you can do is trust *me* with him. Tell him to call me and make an appointment to see me. Explain to him what's going on. It's going to take some time, but time is what we have. Time is running out on you and we have to seal the deal before anything goes further. Forget about the house. Don't even think about trying to live in the house. He's going to make certain that you never have it." She paused to let the ramification of her words sink in.

"I know you're the one who is paying the mortgage now, but if you put the house up for sale, he is not going to make sure the house gets sold for you to get anything out of it. Even if it means he has to burn the house down; he will do whatever it takes to make it happen. Don't be surprised if he doesn't beat you hard enough to where you can't go to work because your pay is paying for mortgage and the bills. Am I right? If you can't go back to work, then you can't pay the mortgage." She paused again, and this time I let the effects of her words sink in through my spirit and soul.

I went home and *he* had returned from his so-called 'visit to his friends in Miami.' *He* appeared to be in good spirits. I was blown away at the incredulity of his wickedness. Not only had he physically, emotionally, and verbally abused me, but now he was set out to destroy me financially. I couldn't believe he really intended not to support his child. It was like the final, ultimate blow. But as I thought about what she said, it made sense. *It's better to have my freedom and my life than to sit around waiting to have a house. What good will a house do me if I'm dead?*

Knowing *him*, based on his past reputation with women, he would have tormented me enough to drive me out of the house. As she had wisely said, men like him don't give up easily. He would taunt and terrorize me; he would even go as far as burning the house down with me in it. She said it clearly: there was *no way* he was going to walk away from that house and leave me in it to live my life without him having any control. Even if the police arrest him for arson, what good would that do if I were dead?

"It's better to get rid of it and move on with your life," she had said ruefully. "Contrary to popular belief, your life will go on."

All these thoughts were running through my head as I drove home. When I got home, I gently broached the subject of credit card debt. A few weeks earlier, there was a commercial on TV about refinancing home mortgages; he suggested we do it to bring down our mortgage payments and our interest rate. I used this as bait.

"Maybe it's time for us to consider that refinancing option we saw a while ago on the TV."

"Yeah," he said, immediately agreeing. "I've been thinking about that because I maxed out all my credit cards and credit card companies won't increase my limits unless I pay off some of it."

"Really?" I said, playing the dumb one. "I didn't know that was going on."

"Yeah! That's why I've been so miserable man," he said, making me his insta-therapist. "I've been so worried about this money thing."

I was thinking *you are such a damn liar. You're not miserable because of that; you're miserable because you're miserable!*

I sat and nodded my head in agreement. "Maybe it's time to refinance," I suggested.

"I've been watching these ads on TV and these people are promising they can give us so much for so little." He seemed as enthusiastic about it as I was.

"Let me go online, look it up, and see if there's truth to it, and we can read the fine print."

"What fine print?" he snapped, allowing that Jekyll/Hyde personality to take hold.

"There's always conditions attached to these things. They're not just going to give the money away for free."

"Oh. Ok." And with that, I got up and went online to look up the company that was advertising on TV. But I had to be careful about the way I went about it because it had to appear to him that he was the one who was in control; if he didn't feel as though he were in control and if he felt control was slipping away from him, then he would lash out and all hopes of this 'plan' working would be gone. I still had to make him feel as though he was in the driver's seat.

So I took him to the computer in the guest room (for I had turned the guest room into a sort of office). Once on the website of the company he mentioned, sure enough the fine print was there. And it wasn't good. On top of that, people had posted reviews of how the company promised to deliver the sun, moon and stars, but once they reached closing, they would ask for hundreds (sometimes thousands) more than they initially asked for.

"These people are nothing but scam artists," he complained.

"Maybe they're not the only ones who do this sort of thing. There's got to be a company around locally who can do this."

"I don't want to deal with the mortgage broker who sold us the house because that guy was a crook."

"Yeah," I said, "I totally agree with you. He was nothing but a slimy, dirty crook."

I started to get into the details of the plan.

"Do you remember the company that gave us the loan to buy my car?" I asked.

"Those people?"

"Yeah!" I answered, a little too eagerly. "They do this kind of thing."

"I didn't know they were into that kind of thing."

"Well, they are, so we can check them out on the Internet, if you'd like…" He agreed and I went to their website.

"Wait a minute," he said, a realization dawning on him. I prayed it wasn't the realization of the plan I was trying to execute.

"This is a bigger company than I thought. I remember financing some furniture through them *years* ago," he said, relief flooding through me. "They're pretty good folks. I didn't know it was them we were dealing with. Maybe we should talk to them about this."

"I don't know if they're still there, but maybe we can find out who is in charge of this sort of thing."

"I don't want to talk to that woman who was there last time. She was rude and nasty to me."

"I don't think she's there anymore," I said. "It's been a year. And maybe she was just having a bad hair day or something. Let me call her and see if we can set this up."

"Yeah, man. There are some things I want to do and I don't have enough credit to do it. And everything is credit-driven these days. It would help me greatly." *It would help me greatly, too.*

And then he got up and walked out of the room. I sat there and wiped invisible sweat from off my brow. *That was easy. How did I get him to agree so quickly?* I shook my head at the thought. *What couldn't happen in one year happened in one day.*

I went to bed that night and for once, I actually looked forward to the morning. The next day dawned bright and early. I was up and as cheery as anything. I was ready to get started on this 'plan' right away. I called up Kathy and told her of the newest development.

"That's wonderful!" she gushed. "Just like that? No quarreling or argument?"

"Just like that," I repeated. "Apparently, he's been wanting to do this for a long time. He agreed to it under one condition: he doesn't want to deal with you again, so we're going to have to find a way to work around that."

"That's fine. Men like him like to work with men. What I'm going to do is have one of my male co-workers call him and set it up. When it comes to closing, I'll make sure I'm there. After that, we can go from there. I'll have John call and befriend him and become his best buddy, then we can get the ball rolling from there."

I called *Sam* back and said, "I just called the office and I have good news. The mean lady you were talking about is on vacation, but they have a guy as her temporary replacement. His name is John, do you want to go see him?"

He asked me to describe what the man looked like. When I was done, he said "Oh! That guy? He's my buddy! Yeah, I'll go see him! Set up a time for me to go see him. When are you off?"

"I'll be off on Tuesday, so you can arrange with him to meet us then."

"That's fine with me," he agreed.

What a boon, I thought. *He doesn't know that guy from anybody else he would see on the street. But because it's a man, he assumes that he is his 'buddy'.* But at the same time, I thought *all things are going to work for my good. I've just got to bide my time.*

Tuesday couldn't have come faster. I was so nervous. I don't know how he couldn't tell I was nervous. For some reason, he kept the peace. There was no quarreling, no shoving, *nothing*. Apparently, he had set his sights on something I couldn't see. Unknown to me, a department store was having a sale on dress shirts and suits. He wanted to buy himself some suits and shirts and needed the extra credit to do it. He just about had the salesman at the store eating out of the palm of his hands. He himself couldn't wait until Tuesday. He even kept asking me about it.

"Do you *really* think we're going to get it? You *really* think it's going to work? You think they'll buy it?"

"I really don't know," I said, acting just as astounded as he. "Let's just hope they will do what we want them to do."

He was as confused and as excited as if he were a child let loose in a candy store.

Tuesday morning finally came. We drove there in separate cars (I'd had nightmares about driving in his car). The last time I drove in his car, he had acted like a crazy man. The only way I could get out of driving in his car and drive in mine was by telling him that I had to go to work afterwards. My real plans were to go to the mall and sit there until my 'shift' was over. I didn't want to spend the day with him alone because I knew it would be awkwardly uncomfortable.

When we got there, just as Kathy had promised, her male co-worker, John met us. *Sam* was in hog heaven. He even went as far as asking if that 'woman' (referring to Kathy) was still here and the entire office replied that she was on vacation and that she wouldn't be back for a while.

John told *him* everything he needed to hear. The one thing he didn't tell him was that my car would be paid off.

"Let me see the documents," he demanded after a while.

When he saw my car was listed as one of the debts to be paid off, he almost went crazy.

"*Her* car is going to be paid off?"

"Yes," John responded calmly. "It's part of the debt you have acquired. If you include the car in it, you'd be able to pay off everything you owe and you could live free. Just imagine how much money you would have in your pocket every month if she didn't make a car payment every month. You could go on vacation more often, you could go shopping more often, all those nice things you'd been missing out on because of *her*."

"I never knew her car would be involved in the deal," *he* lamented.

"But look at this way: when you're married, you want her to be happy. Because if she's happy, then you're happy. Just think: you could be free to do whatever else you wanted to. You could even trade up that car if you wanted to and get a nicer, better one."

"Yeah," he said. "I could get a nicer Chrysler or even a Cadillac one day."

"That's true," John agreed. "You wouldn't get a lot of anything for your car, but for her car you could get much, much more. If you pay it off, you could own it."

Much to my surprise, *Sam* agreed. And then he signed. I didn't believe it.

I was holding my breath, waiting for something bad to happen. And something did happen, in my favor, at that. The tension in the room was so palpable that you could have walked in there and sliced a knife through it.

When he signed it, I let out an audible breath of air.

"What happened?" he asked, looking at me strangely.

"Nothing," I said, playing it off.

I didn't know what to do; I was so giddy with excitement. It was now guaranteed that we would get the loan. It was guaranteed that my car would be paid off. But he signed it and there wasn't a damn thing he could do about it. There was nothing more to it.

I looked at the document and thought *this is really going to happen. I'm going to be free.*

As we left the office he said, "Wow, John sure was a nice guy, wasn't he? That's a man. That's how a man should be, always taking care of business. He promised me he would take care of this and he did just that."

"Yeah, it certainly seems he's going to work things out in our favor," I agreed smiling. "I have to go to work, so I'll see you later." I got in my car and drove off.

I dared not look back out of fear he would see my Cheshire cat grin. I prayed he would drive off and not go back in the office and change his mind. I just kept driving north. I picked up my cell phone and dialed the office of the finance company. I was holding my breath, when Kathy answered the call.

"I was here in my office the entire time," she said, the smile creeping through her voice. "I had the door closed and I was in here and I heard *everything*. It's going to be all right now. I just need to submit this to my supervisor for approval and that will take a couple of days. But I promise it's going to be all right. Just hang in there because it's almost over!"

For the first time since the horrid days of my marriage had begun, I started to feel hopeful. I drove to a restaurant, ordered lunch, and sat down to enjoy it by myself.

The next few days passed by in a blur. Sam was literally hanging on to hope the credit cards would be paid off. He called John back himself repeatedly over the next few days to make sure everything was going fine. He even called the credit card companies to tell them what was about to happen. He was so excited about paying off all the debt. He even suggested upon receiving the money, we make improvements at the house.

It took all of ten days for the approval to come. For some reason, it seemed longer.

"Here's the deal," Kathy said to me after the approval came. "When the car loan is paid off and the title comes, it's going to come to your house. If it comes to your house, he can hold the title. Get a P.O. Box from the post office and list that as your address. We'll mail the car title to the P.O. Box so that *he* can't have access to it."

When the title came, I had my P.O. Box secured. I placed the title to the car in my hand luggage secured by a set of combination locks, as well as my passport and all important documents relating to me until I could give them to a friend for safe-keeping. Just in case something happened, *he* wouldn't have access to them.

By the time the official letter came in the mail, *he* was beside himself with happiness. But then he started to have second thoughts about why it happened the way it did. Somehow, he started to believe it was setup. I knew I was going to pay for it.

He started to think I was getting away with something. When he realized he was not only paying off *my* credit cards, but I was getting my car *paid* for, he was furious. He requested to go back up to the finance company and cancel the loan. By this time, it was too late; he had already signed it.

He called the finance company, and Kathy answered the phone.

"What are you doing there? I thought you were on vacation! My wife cuckolded that man (John) into talking me into signing that thing and now I'm having second thoughts."

"Sir, your wife didn't convince you or John to do anything. You voluntarily came here of your own free will and signed it. It's already a done deal and your first payment will be due shortly. If you don't pay it, then the company will have to take over the house."

I didn't know this conversation had taken place. I came home and wondered why he had been calling me all day and asking what time I would be getting home. When I got home, he was eerily quiet. *Something must be wrong*, I thought.

Sure enough, something *was* wrong. I could feel the waves of anger coming through the garage door when I got home. He was sitting on the couch watching TV, but not all too interested in what was actually on the TV. I dropped my keys and said hi. He just turned and looked at me. That look he gave me was enough. I debated internally whether or not I should go into the bedroom. I tried to think of what I should do because I knew the time had come. I just stood there and waited on him to come and hit me.

He got up and said, "How did you come up with the idea of refinancing a loan on the house?"

"What?" I was confused.

"Who told you to do that?"

"What do you mean?"

"Whose idea was it?"

I didn't answer because I didn't know *how* to answer.

"You can't answer, can you?" he said. "You and that bitch at the finance company set me up. What did you do with my money?"

"What are you talking about it?" In truth, I hadn't done anything with his money.

"You and that bitch set me up! You and her got together to gang up on me. I should call up there and have her lose her damn job. Do you know I can do that? You and her set me up to rob me of my money."

"How did anyone rob you of your money? You never *paid* any money."

"No, I didn't pay any money, but I'm about to lose my money in this house. I signed a deal for your f---- car to be paid off."

He kept on ranting and swearing. I was trying to walk past him and he grabbed me in my throat and slammed me up against the stainless steel refrigerator.

"Please, don't," I started to beg.

"Please don't *what?* I'm going to beat the truth out of you."

He backhanded me across my face twice and pushed me. I got away from him and started running towards the bedroom. I ran into the bedroom, shut and locked the door.

He was at the door before I could blink.

"OPEN THIS ----&&&?? --- DOOR BEFORE I KICK IT DOWN YOU DIRTY BITCH!" he screamed. I felt he would actually kick the door down with his brute strength. "IF YOU DON'T OPEN THIS DOOR, I'M GONNA *KILL* YOU!"

I heard Alex come out of her room and say, "Daddy, if you say one more word, I'm going to scream for the neighbors to call the police." That's what did him in. He walked away from the door.

I stood behind the door shaking. I was so afraid to open the door because I didn't know if he was still standing there. Finally, I opened the door when my daughter said "Mommy, it's me, it's ok to open the door now." When I opened the door, she came in and sat beside me.

"I can't wait for this to be over," I whispered to her. I felt like everything in my body was tightly wound up. I called my mother the next day and told her how badly I had to get out of the situation. She agreed with me and asked to speak to *him*. My daughter took the phone to him and told him whom it was.

"What do you want?" he angrily asked into the receiver.

"Don't talk to me like that! You're down there abusing my daughter and my granddaughter and you didn't give birth to them. Who told you that you had that right?"

I sat there thinking the time has to come for me to leave.

12
Leaving

After that incident, I knew time was running out. Now as I look back on it, it became apparent there were key factors pointing to the beginning of the end of my marriage. It was clear to me that something had to be done.

I think *he*, having more wisdom than I did, must have seen it, too. I think he, too, might have been making preparations. I just didn't see it because I was too caught up in trying to survive. I now believe the money he took to go 'shopping' he probably gave to one of his friends and told them to hold it for him. He had already raped me physically; now he was raping me financially.

It is important for women and others in this situation to know this is part of the system of abuse. The abuser will never let you walk away with enough of anything left. Not only will he rob you of your self esteem, he will set out to systematically destroy you emotionally and rob you of your freedom, alienate and isolate you, create such emotional disturbance that you cannot work and condemn you to poverty, cementing your dependence on him. I could not begin to imagine the extent of depravity this man had brought to my life. It took years for me to recover from the after-effects of verbal and emotional trauma he brought to my life.

The abuser will also make sure to withdraw all money he has access to from your joint account. In my case, more than twenty-five thousand dollars went missing. I just couldn't see it as I was too busy trying to dodge his fists and playing hit and miss from fiery darts of his words.

It's safe to say alienation and isolation form part of an abuse cycle. You will find yourself being alienated from friends and family, and isolated from contact with anyone outside of his close inner circle. For most women, initially this seems flattering to them, as they believe it to be a sign of him caring. But what you can't see and he won't allow you to see is the noose he is tightening around you by robbing you of any independent contact of anyone that might aid you in escaping from him in the future. I have often told women to be careful of the man who tries to influence whom you are friendly with and whom you talk to. Don't, for one-minute, mistake his attempts at controlling your conversation and interactions with friends to mean he cares for you. In fact what he 's doing is setting up a carefully constructed system of only his contacts so you will never be able to escape.

By its nature, abuse renders a woman incapable of trusting anyone else. So she finds it difficult to form relationships with new persons.

The shame associated with physical battering is often more than she can bear. It is demeaning to stand before an adult to confide your husband hits you with his fists or uses his belt to chase you around the house. It's almost frightening to the human adult mind to be reduced to the helpless state of a child disciplined by a parent. This was the situation I found myself in. I was trying with the broken emotional equipment I had, using the scenarios I just explained to find a way to escape the fire I had been living through. I was damaged emotionally; I knew it; and I knew I had to get help. Deep in my mind, I knew when this was over some serious therapy sessions would have to take place in order to become whole.

My car being paid off became a bone of contention with him. He could never get over the feeling he had been duped into doing something he wouldn't profit from. It didn't matter his credit card debt exceeded what I owed on the car. It didn't matter his credit cards were now free and clear and he could do whatever he wanted with them. What mattered to him was now I would have freedom to leave, and that was the one thing he didn't want.

My home had become a prison. I couldn't stay in it, but I couldn't get out of it. The more I tried to get out of it, the tighter the lines became. It didn't seem to matter anymore what he did. I had developed a thick skin when it came to the shoving and pushing. Since the time my daughter threatened she would scream and call the police, he would never hit me enough for her to scream; he would just push and shove.

Every evening when I came home, he would confront me and accuse me of cheating on him and being a whore. He would accuse me of being a whore so badly; I would start to wonder if he'd ever seen what a real whore looks like. *If I were whoring like he said I was, I would have tons more money. What would I need him for then?* It was ludicrous. I was an upstanding member of the community, working, paying my taxes, paying my bills, going to church and doing what any law-abiding citizen does, and here comes this man accusing me of being a *whore*?

Why? You're the one who raped me and now *you're* the one accusing me of being a whore. It seemed to me he figured out the worst thing he could ever accuse me of was the one thing that could completely decimate me.

I just resigned myself to the fact I had to go.

He decided the time had come for the little money we had left in the bank to be solely his property. There was now $10,000 left after his 'shopping spree'. Then he said he needed to do some repairs on his car, which would cost $3,000;

I gave it to him. Now there was only $7,000 left. He insisted that he wanted that little $7,000 and if I didn't give it to him, he was going to kill me.

I never believed in any of his threats of coming to the office. But one day while I was at work, he showed up. Security had to escort him out of the building. That infuriated him to no end. Human resources called me and told me he insisted on seeing me, and when they said no, he became uncontrollable and they had to remove him from the building. Going home that day felt like going home to a nightmare.

I went home that night with great trepidation and I believed I was going to be beaten. As I drove home, I pictured me ending up on the six o'clock news the next day with the headline *Battered Wife Found Dead in Home*; they would run the video of my bloody, beaten and lifeless body being transported to the emergency vehicle in a body bag. I imagined what life would be like for my daughter. Alex would be left without a mother *and* without a father even though that title was one he did not deserve. I did not have the controls to stop what would come that evening.

My marriage had become a cesspool of worry, anxiety, tension and fear. It had become so my clothes swam on me because I never ate. I whittled down to skin and bones. As I drove home, I was hoping and praying for a miracle.

When I got home, he met me inside the kitchen before I barely gathered my bearings.

"I have one thing to tell you," he said, smugly standing at the kitchen counter. "I want my mother---- money or I'm going to kill you. Tomorrow morning, if you don't go up to that f----- bank and bring my money, I'm going to go that worthless place you work and drag you out kicking and screaming and kill you. Do you understand me?" Before I could answer, he walked away.

That was my breaking point. As I stood there and watched him walk away, I thought, *this is it*. I went to lie down and try to sleep, but I couldn't. The tension in the atmosphere was entirely too palpable. I didn't know if he would come in the room to try to kill me there or if he would wait until first light. I slept with a steak knife under my pillow so I could feel some semblance of protection. I prayed he wouldn't come near me.

It was like living with an intruder in your house. It felt like I was constantly at war; I knew the enemy was coming so I had to prepare myself mentally for it. All that constant mental preparation and anticipation wears a person out after a while. And so you sleep with the weapons of war and have them ready to draw, just like a soldier always has his knife or his gun ready to kill. That's what my marriage was like. It was a perpetual state of war that unleashed its destructive effects upon my daughter and me.

We had no other place to go and live; we had no one who could help us. I was an undocumented resident of the country and I had no way of proving myself legal. My immigration situation was up in the air. And *he* was the one who would determine the course of my life.

The next morning I got up and went to work. I filed a complaint and told everyone there to expect him. As soon as I walked in, the first person I saw was not the receptionist, but the Human Resources Manager, who was a very kind lady. She took one look at me and knew something was wrong.

"Honey, is there any way I can help you?" she asked.

"Yes," I said, "I need to speak with my supervisor."

"She's not here yet. But are you sure there isn't anything I can do to help?"

I knew she was trying to get something out of me, but I was so ashamed of what I was going through. I didn't want anyone else to know because I felt they would fire me if they knew what was going on with me. I desperately needed the job. I told her I didn't trust anyone and I just kept clinging to the belief everything would be ok, if I saw my supervisor.

"Sweetie, I can help you. Just let me help," was all she could say after looking in my face.

"Would you please tell my supervisor I need to see her as soon as possible?"

"Yes," she said dejectedly. "Let me take you to the lounge." She placed her hand around my shoulders and walked me to the lounge.

That was my breaking point. That was the straw that broke my back. When she showed up, I said, "I'm so sorry, but I can't work today." She just looked at me.

"We knew this day would come."

"How?" I asked.

"We know abuse is taking place in your home."

I burst into tears. I told her how he had threatened me he would come to work that day and kill me if I didn't give him the money. I think I may have told them everything. Those two ladies just sat there and listened to me.

"I'm so sorry, but we knew this was coming. Another woman who works beside you has been through this before and she knew what to tell us. We've been watching for some time."

"I don't know what else to do!" I exclaimed between sobs.

"Do you have any family in the area?" they asked.

"No," I said.

"Here's what's going to help. You need to go to counseling and we're going to set you up to do so. If you go to counseling, then you'll be able to figure out what you need to do from there. So go to counseling."

They made some phone calls and set me up to undergo therapeutic counseling. Once I had an appointment, they told me to take the rest of the day off.

"But I have no place to go," I protested.

"Go somewhere. Forget about it for today. You're in no condition to work today."

The money from this job was the only money I had left. I recognized now *he* totally and completely intended to destroy me. He had no intention of ever providing for my daughter. And he never had any intention of providing for me, either. He realized there were certain things he couldn't control anymore. He couldn't control that I was working, but he was wise enough to foresee I would leave him eventually.

To me, the abuse was intentional. He intentionally abused me physically, emotionally and verbally. And now, the final abusive straw was the financial one. But I was going to get out of it, even if I only got out with my car. After 13 years of marriage, the only thing I was going to walk away with was a car. A car that would, over time, depreciate and have no value. But at least it would provide me with the freedom and mobility to move.

I went to the bank, and with a heavy heart, I asked them to give me the remaining funds that were in the account in a check written in *his* name. And I took the check and gave it to him.

"Here is your money. Are you happy now?"

"I'm fine."

He took the check and didn't say another word.

13
Done

I began therapy and it proved to be the one thing that helped me to survive the abuse typifying my life. Once I began a series of sessions with the therapist, it began to expose the lies that surrounded my life. It started to tear down the barriers and walls I had erected as safekeeping around me. Because of the intentional emotional and verbal abuse, I was *this* close to actually believing the things *he* said about me. Therapy began to expose the things he said about me as the lies they were.

Word by word, I was able to obliterate every lie that man had ever told. It was important for me to identify within myself the key areas he attacked and to see myself as a victor and as an over-comer in those areas. I would one day fulfill all the plans for my life I had been created to do.

Everyone has a calling. I was nowhere near reaching mine. I began to realize, through therapy, this wicked fiery furnace of a marriage was just *one* aspect of my life. This is an important realization for anyone going through abuse. You must begin to imagine a life after abuse and focus on the good that will reflect the remainder of your life. This is what I have been telling myself all these years, is that *my best days are ahead*, in fact on my face book page my favorite quotation is "The best is yet to come".

Abuse didn't encompass my entire life. I wasn't born to be abused, I wasn't created to be abused, and I wasn't called to be abused. It was simply a fact of life that had happened to me. Nothing more, nothing less. And now, I was able to reverse the effects of it.

It was a revealing moment for me. It was an entrancing moment. It was a moment in time in which I learned to verbalize, from my own mouth, what happened during that marriage. It was important for me to say the words out loud and to hear myself say them. Not only was verbalization therapeutic, it was healing. There were deep emotional wounds violated in this marriage.

As more lies surfaced through therapy, it became more evident I had to get out of this marriage and be done with it, once and for all. I realized the stage for my being done had already been set with me being given my financial freedom. While money was important, I came to view it as just a tool. Money was just a currency, a piece of paper that I could hold in my hand. It could come, and it could go.

While he destroyed me financially and took every last penny out of our account, the one thing he didn't destroy was *I,* and all of me at that. He didn't destroy me physically and he didn't destroy me emotionally. He might have destroyed me financially, but time heals those wounds.

My therapist described scenarios of other women who had been through the same thing and survived. She told me the only way I was going to get out of it was by confronting it. If I didn't confront it, then I would *never* be done with it.

"How do I confront it?" I asked.

"You're going to have to be proactive and take charge of the situation."

"How do I do that?"

"Each time he hits you, because you fear being deported, you never call the police. That is an unrealistic fear. Let me tell you why: there is a law called the Violence Against Women's Act. Because there is an established precedence of this man being violent towards you, you can never be deported. What you need is a good attorney who will file a case for you based on the evidence presented by the police reports, evidence from your therapy sessions, and evidence provided by your employer. The evidence will say this man has cultivated an atmosphere of violence and note his violence was prejudiced against you. *Trust* me when I say you will never be deported. Until you know this truth, you, and women like you, just sit in situations like this and do nothing about it."

I was stunned. *Had I known this*, I thought, *that sucker would be rotting away in a prison cell*. Unbelievable, I thought. What you don't know certainly does hurt you. All the years of being hit and being emotionally battered could have been avoided had I known this one fact. And to think he had carefully selected the immigration attorney. He made sure to choose one whom he could manipulate into doing exactly what he wanted. No way would that guy have exposed me to this emancipated truth. My goodness, I thought, each time I think he couldn't sink lower, he did. What on earth did I do to this man for him to treat me like this? This thought kept swirling around my mind.

The more time I spent in therapy, I was presented with a profile of an abuser. I was stunned at the actual resemblance between Sam and the generic description and similarities between the profile and the Sam. Looking back, I recalled conversations I overheard amongst his family and friends. In these conversations, the women of his past also seemed to follow a pattern. Every one of them had been treated the same as I. So the blame was not '*what had I done to deserve this*'; I had been caught in a carefully set trap that a scheming and clever man had set to capture his victims.

For you to understand what abuse is, you have to clearly understand who is the victim. The victim does not choose to be a victim. The abuser is the dominant person who is the master of the game. Sam had been mastering his game of abuse and had developed some success with it for quite some time. The difficulty I experienced in finding out about I before it was too late, was the secrecy, his friends and family members did to cover it up. Had I not gone through it myself I would never have known. In fact, when I tried unsuccessfully through friends and family to determine what caused him to be so violent, I was met with much resistance; no one wanted to open up, which is typical of abusive men and their families to cover up any character traits that would identify them as being out of control. Nobody would open up. However it is clear that no one is born violent. Physical and emotional violence is a learned behavior. Sam had to have been exposed to it to learn this was the way males in a family setting should express their desire for control over their female family members.

I thought back to an incident that took place a few months ago. Because *he* had proceeded to file documents for my attaining a green card, I received a letter in the mail from the immigration authorities that I was to present myself at their offices for an interview for my green card. When we arrived there, the man who was the interviewing officer, who sat across from me, presented a letter *Sam* had written to immigration authorities some time back. Prior to me arriving there, I had never heard of nor seen this letter, and I did not know of its existence.

In that letter, *he* stipulated quite clearly I had every intention of leaving him and taking his daughter out of the country if I were to ever be granted a green card. He also said that he was the American citizen and I had only married him to obtain a green card just so I could take his child and run away. If I were granted this freedom, he claimed, then he would never see nor hear from his child again.

Of course, all of those things were lies; I didn't know what the naturalization/processing procedure was like in the country. But that's what he alleged in the letter. At the time we had been married, we lived outside the United States in a country and society where I was well established; in fact at the time, he himself had not been naturalized, and had no intention of doing so. So this, to me and to him, was a lie.

Had I known he said these things in the letter, or he even wrote the letter, I would have brought the police report and the injunction I filed evidencing the abuse. I had no idea this was coming. *He* had traveled with me to the offices, knowing he wrote the letter and knowing there was no chance in hell I *wouldn't* find out about it.

When the officer presented the letter, he showed it to *him* first and asked if that was his writing and his signature. *He* responded yes to both questions. The attorney that was sitting beside me was also part of the scam. In fact, *he* had originally sent the letter to the attorney, who then sent it to the immigration office.

As I sat there, I could only stare at him.

"So, sir," I said to the gentleman, "my life is in your hands."

"Yes it is," he agreed. "But I have to believe the words of your husband."

"But, how could you believe that?" I asked, astounded. "I didn't come to this country until we'd been married for almost ten years. So why would it take me all that time to take my daughter out of the country? Wouldn't I have done it already?"

"But ma'am, *he's* the citizen."

"So you choose to believe the words of an abusive man? Did he tell you how many times he beat me? Did he tell you how many times he has shoved and kicked me?"

"Well, that is not for me to judge," said the gentleman.

I was flabbergasted by now.

"But you are judging *me* based on *his* word. Is this an exclusive old boy's club? You only believe the words of the man? You don't believe my words? Here is our daughter; ask her. By the way, did he tell you this is *his* daughter? Ask her what has happened in the marriage."

"Ma'am, it's not our place to speak to children," he said coldly. I was now convinced this man had no heart.

"But you're accusing me and not giving me a chance to defend myself. You're taking *his* word for it."

"Well, since *he*'s here now, he can speak for himself." *Amazing*, I thought, *you'd let him speak for himself, but not me?*

"Did you write that letter?" I asked *him*.

"Yes," he said, unashamed.

"If you knew you wrote the letter, why did you tell me to come here today? You knew there was no chance in hell they would process me after reading that. So why did you write those lies?"

No answer.

I turned to the 'officer ' and said "Now what? Where do I go from here?"

"I can't process you," he said after a long pause.

"Why not? That letter in front of you gives you all the more reason to process me. You have the power to give me freedom, so then why won't you just let me have it?"

"No, I'm not going to." *Evil son of a bitch. I hope you get shot, fall in the ocean, and eaten alive by a shark.*

"Why not?"

"Because, ma'am, I can't."

"Don't you ma'am me! Why not?"

"Ma'am, you do realize I have the power to deport you, right?"

"*Deport* me? On what grounds? *Why? He* didn't give me a Visa to enter the country. I didn't do anything wrong and I haven't done anything wrong. You're simply taking the words of an abusive man over mine. If I go home right now, I could flood your office with evidence of abuse."

"The only thing I can do is return you to your current jurisdiction and let them deal with it."

I was now absolutely sure this man had no heart, no feelings and no emotion. And judging by the finality of his tone, he had already made up his mind and there was no changing it. There were a few words I could say.

"Sir," I said, on the verge of getting on my knees and begging, "Look at me carefully. I want you to remember my name, because one day, it's going to be in lights. And I want you to remember what you have done to me because what you've done is condemn me to live at the request of *that* man, who has the power to kill me. But you're going to *remember* me and remember my face and my name. It's going to haunt you for as long as you live."

That was the end of that.

As we walked out of the immigration offices, I felt as though the walls of my marriage had just about crumbled. I couldn't believe he had been so cruel to do that to me. Once we walked out of the office, the attorney disappeared and I never saw him again.

The legal ramifications of what happened that day were still unfathomable to me. My daughter had been sitting there the entire time and had to witness the whole thing. Unknown to *him*, what he did to me not only affected me, but affected her as well. Now, I would never get a green card. I would have to go back through the system and reapply, not knowing how I could or would reapply and under what petitions I could reapply. This was August of 2000 and that moment was one of the most devastating of my life. It was like *he* had built a trap for me to fall into.

I'm remembering all of this while sitting in the therapist's office. When I told her all of this, she said "What your attorney didn't know (and it's a good thing he didn't know) was that you can get away by filing a petition under the Violence Against Women's Act. The evidence for you is so overwhelming, your application could *never* be turned down."

I sat back in my chair. I felt as if someone had just attached wings to my arms and I could now fly.

Some pop star sang a song with the lyrics "I believe I can fly…" I literally felt as though I could. This woman sitting across from me was giving me every reason to no longer stay in that loveless marriage. With all the abuse that was going on, I never called the police because I feared if they came, because I had no legal status (except a driver's license), they would remove me from the country and leave my daughter in *his* care. And that was the one thing I feared most: leaving her behind. And *he knew* I had that fear and he used it every time he hit me. And he continually used it to engage in physical and emotional abuse to condemn me and keep me trapped.

But, yet and still, here I was, being given wings to fly. That was the single most liberating moment of that part of my life. I finally looked at the situation and was ready to face all it took to leave the situation.

I went home and ruminated over all that went on in the therapy session. I didn't say anything about the session to *him*. I am quite sure when a man places a woman in a position where he has robbed her of every decency, robbed her of her dignity, violated her personally, and violated her financially, he has literally caused her to be like an animal who has been pushed into a corner. Depending on how strong her drive is to live, she will live, at all costs. And that was true in my case.

I had found my drive to live. I was now fully convinced I was going to get out of this somehow. I didn't know how long it was going to take for me to be approved under that petition, but in October of 2000, I determined whatever it took for me to get out of this is what I would do.

The stronghold *he* had over me where he used this legal processing battle to hold me captive was broken. Now I was ready to fight back.

Not only had I been given wings to fly; I had been given back my fighting spirit. The tiger in me had now come out and I was beyond ready to take on my husband Goliath. I was now on a mission to take back my dignity; take back my emotions that had been violated; take back my life that had been stolen from me. The next time he would raise his hand against me in terror, I would not run, but I would stand there and bear it. And the same force he used in his fists is the same force with which I would use the Justice system to come after him, when calling the police on his sorry ass.

Since I couldn't physically fight him back, I would join forces with those who had the power to silence him (the local authorities). Sitting in that therapist's office, I got my fight back.

I was no longer going to sit back and be a bystander to my own life. I was no longer going to sit back and let him walk all over me, abuse me, beat me, push and shove me just because he felt he had a right to do so. I was going to *take* it back. I was born to be a winner. I was born to be an over-comer. When my mother gave birth to me, she didn't birth me for some *lowlife* like *him* to abuse me. I was now going to make *sure* I got back everything that had been stolen from me. Just as he was hell-bent on destroying me, I was hell-bent on winning.

I walked out of that therapist's office like a prized boxing champion about to enter the ring. My entire demeanor changed. I no longer looked at the ground when I walked. I lifted up my head and pushed my shoulders back and strutted to my car. I got in my car with the assurance *something* had to give.

14
Finished

One of the things I like to do when I'm stressed is go for long drives. In those days, you could drive for miles without fear of reproach. We lived in a suburb north of the city of Orlando and there were many nice communities around with lots of rolling, beautiful countryside. One of the things I liked to do before I went home was put miles on my car driving through these areas, enjoying the vistas of rolling hills and beautifully landscaped lawns. It was relieving for me and provided me some level of relaxation.

I felt I now had become empowered by the information my therapist shared with me. Her words changed my view of my circumstances forever. I was no longer a person without hope. I was now a person filled with purpose. Now that I knew the truth, the truth would operate to my benefit. Because a vicious falsification had been perpetrated on me, I sat in that marriage and endured the abuse because I felt I had no legal recourse. *That* was a lie. Once I went to therapy and that lie was exposed, it was time to fight back.

There is an old saying, "you can win the battle, but you won't win the war." It wasn't the war *he* had won; it was just the battle. The war was mine for the taking.

This particular day I was driving around, trying to achieve some peace in my mind. I knew the time was coming for the end. It was truly like being in a war, where you and your enemy have skirmishes. But there is a bigger fight at hand you know is going to come. So, you prepare yourself mentally and emotionally for it.

I decided to drive to the mall. I parked my car and was sitting in my car when I started thinking, *how many times am I going to sit in a parking lot at the mall because I don't want to go home? How many times am I going to sleep in my car? People will soon start to think I live in my car.* I turned the car on, backed out of the parking space and drove to my hairstylist.

Getting my hair done was another of my relaxation methods. *Sam* called, "Where are you? What are you doing out so long?"

"I'm at the hairdresser," I answered, calm as ever. "I'm getting my hair done. I'll be home when I'm ready." Then I hung up the phone.

He wasn't expecting that. He was used to me placating him and succumbing to whatever he wanted me to do.

He didn't say anything when I got home. He was quiet. I changed my clothes and was watching TV. He was just sitting on the couch. All of a sudden, it was as if something came over him. He started quarrelling about nothing in particular. I didn't say a word. As the hour got later, the more he quarreled and the more I didn't say anything. After a while, I got tired of hearing his voice and decided to go sit in the living room to look at the sky through the sunroof that was in the ceiling. He didn't like that. And he didn't like the fact that I was ignoring him.

He got up, walked over to me, grabbed me by my hair and yanked me up out of the chair. That short gesture enraged me. He didn't even have the decency to at least yell at me to come sit on the couch with him; he just felt it necessary to yank me up by my hair and drag me over there. My head was tender because I had just had my hair done. The hairdresser had used the blow dryer and the flat iron so my scalp was still tender. He grabbed me with such force I thought he had lifted my scalp from off my head.

"Didn't you hear me call you?" he asked. "I said come now!"

"What are you calling me for? And why are you yanking my head? Let me go!" I demanded.

"Bitch! Who told you to talk to me like that?"

"Take your hands off me and let me go!" I was just as furious as he was.

"Bitch – "

"Do not EVER call me a bitch! Take your hands off me and let me go NOW!"

He slapped me across my face.

"That's enough," I said. "I've HAD it!"

"What are you talking about enough?"

"I said that's ENOUGH and I've HAD IT!"

And I ran to my daughter's room to get the telephone to dial 911. It took him a second to realize what I was doing. As I ran towards the room, I yelled to her "Grab the phone and dial 911!" She heeded my call immediately, picked up the phone, giving it to me. In mere milliseconds, I dialed 911. He ran to the room and yanked at my ankles to try to drag me away from the phone.

But I heard the operator say, "911, what's your emergency?" I quickly yelled my address into the phone and explained my husband was beating me up. At that point, he snatched the phone from me and yanked the phone out of the wall jack.

He threw me against the wall, then he threw the phone at me and it hit me on the side of my face. I rolled over on the bed trying to run out of the room. He grabbed me and slammed me into the doorpost with immense force. I kicked at him and said "Didn't I tell you not to put your hands on me? Don't you EVER put your hands on me!"

I ran to the master bedroom and slammed the door.

My daughter stood in the living room and started to elicit a deafening, ear-splitting scream. "I'm going to scream until the neighbors call the police! I want you to stop hitting my mother NOW!" Alex screamed loudly, I expected glass to shatter.

He grabbed the phone in his hand and tried to break it. He didn't know once you dial 911, they immediately use caller id to track the source of the call. And considering I told them my address and what was going on, they probably had a police unit on the way. It was probably worse because they heard a screaming child in the background.

The doorbell rang and two sheriff deputies were there. When the doorbell rang, he didn't know what to do because he didn't want to be the one to answer the door. I cracked opened the door of the bedroom and saw my daughter standing in the middle of the living room and *he* was standing there in his pajamas. I looked at him and smiled.

When I opened the door, the sheriff deputy looked at me, looked at *him*, and *he* had the nerve to try and be social by inviting them in.

The officers, ignoring his casual manner, walked in. "We received a phone call so we came to see if everything is alright."

He said, "Everything is alright. Nothing is wrong." One of them was black and the other was white. He immediately developed an affinity for the black guy. The deputy looked at me point blank and asked "Ma'am is everything alright?"

"No," I answered. "No, it's not. My husband hit me."

"The bitch is lying, man!" *he* started. "I'm telling you about these bitches, man. All they do is make up stories about a brother and lie, man."

The black deputy said, "Sir, would you mind stepping outside?"

"Sure," he said. "Yeah, I'm telling you about these bitches man; they're liars! I picked up this piece of shit on the side of the road and put her in my house and now she's telling lies on me."

The two deputies looked at each other and smiled.

The deputy who stayed inside with me turned to my daughter and said "Sweetheart, I want you to tell me what happened."

"Daddy is always hitting mommy and I'm tired of it. I told Daddy I was going to scream until neighbors called the police to come and rescue my mommy." That was all he needed to hear.

The deputy turned to me and said "Ma'am, did he hit you?"

"Yes he did." I turned my face to show him the scratch that was a result of him throwing the phone at me.

They saw it and determined that was all they needed to book him. They read him his rights and right there, in front of my daughter and I, arrested him. They packed him in the back of the police cruiser and they took off.

I could not believe that was the end of my nightmare of a marriage. I couldn't believe the marriage ended that night, just like that. One phone call was all it took. The Power of a phone call, all my hopes for this nightmare to end took only one phone call to bring it to an end. My, my, my. What a release.

Not until the therapist gave me the application and gave me the truth to uncover the lies this man had perpetrated against me did I really become free. That was what set in motion a series of events that would lead to my ultimate freedom. With one phone call, I was able to completely obliterate that lie. One phone call freed me more than anything else could have ever done.

That night, I was in peace. They arrested him, locked him up and took him away. *In his pajamas!* That was what took the cake. I could stand there and watch him be led away knowing that would be the last time he and I would ever live in a house together. Never, never, *never* again would we be in a house together. That marriage was over and that life was over.

As he was led away, all I could do was look at him. *Now look at that*, I thought, *the blood that he tried to seal this marriage with was the same blood he was walking away with* (his pajamas were red). Just like the red he had always liked. Just like my own blood that he had shed on numerous occasions.

As I looked at it, I was so glad it was over. I couldn't believe I was finally free.

I went to bed that night. It was sort of anti-climactic after he left. Because now that he was physically gone, I had to rid myself of the emotional residue he left behind. I had to sit down and really process the fact he would never come back. I even called the sheriff's office to find out if he was going to come back that night. They told me no; he had to be processed first and he had to post bail and none of that would be taken care of until the morning. They also politely informed me that he would be sleeping in a jail cell that night.

They also told me that a victim's rights' advocate would come to see me the next day and inform me on what the next course of events would be. All night, I did not sleep. I sat up all night thinking about my newfound freedom. I was so accustomed to tossing and turning all night that it was normal for me to just sit there and stay up.

I didn't realize the extent to which I had been emotionally damaged. I had no idea what would be coming down the pike in the next coming days. I stayed up all-night and sat in the family room with the TV turned off, staring at the screen. The first person I called was my mother. "Thank God," she said, her voice cracking with relief. But, it wasn't quite over yet.

As dawn broke, I realized it was truly the dawn of a new day for me. The nightmare was over and *finished*. Suddenly, the struggle was really over. It was a new day filled with new hopes and a new life. It was time for me to begin that day. I was as free as a bird. Now it was just a matter of time for the rest to work out. The question was no longer *now what?* The question (or command) was *next!*

I used to dream when the end finally did come, it would be a cinema-like moment where I just walked off into sunset. But nothing prepared me for how I felt. It was as if I were frozen in place. I couldn't move from the couch. I looked around the family room that had become his habitat. We had lived in that house for approximately ten months and not one night did we sleep in the same bed. As I looked around the family room, I saw all of his personal effects: his wallet, his medication, his reading glasses, his sunglasses, and his keys; I realized that he really was never coming back to this house.

I felt like getting up and throwing everything of his into the trash. I wanted to rid the place of any trace of his presence. I thought if I could remove him physically from my life, then I could remove the memory of him. As I looked at his stuff, a nasty taste brimmed in the back of my mouth and I felt bile rise up in my stomach into my throat. I ran to the bathroom to throw up. As I heaved into the toilet, I felt as if I was purging myself of the memory of what he had done to me. I was so sick with the very thought of him. I told myself it was going to be all right and I was to calm down. I washed my face off and went back to the living room.

As I walked through the living room, I saw the footprints the officers had left from the night before. I considered cleaning them, but then I put them off saying *I will eventually get around to it*.

I walked into the kitchen and what he made for dinner from the night before was still on the stove. I took that pot and everything in it and threw it in the trash. I opened the garage door and I took everything that was in the fridge he had touched and I put it all in the garbage bags and threw it in the garbage can at the end of the driveway.

As I walked back into the family room, a second wave of understanding hit me. I couldn't go to work. As free as I was, the scars he gave me left me emotionally devastated. I had nothing left in me. I couldn't function or respond to an outside person's needs at that point. I couldn't even talk. So I called in sick and told them what had happened. I also told them I would be filling a police report.

Next, I called my therapist and filled her in and she congratulated me.

My daughter started to get ready for school. I walked her to the bus stop, gave her a hug and a kiss, told her how much I loved her, and sent her off to school. And then I was alone.

The doorbell rang and I wondered how I was now going to deal with the resulting legal implications. It was the victim's advocate from the sheriff's office. I met her and escorted her to the living room, inviting her to sit down. As soon as she sat down, I burst into tears.

"It's ok," she consoled me in a gentle voice. "It's normal for you to cry."

"Where do I go from here?" I asked.

She explained the justice system to me. I would have to file an injunction for protection from him. He was going to be taken to court and she advised me I shouldn't be there because him seeing me seeing him in chains would infuriate him more. There began the legal process.

I had no money to hire a lawyer because he had already ensured I had no money at all. I later found out he called somebody who would post bail for him, but they couldn't get to him for a few days. For those few days, he sat in jail. And that infuriated him to no end. It was good for me, though. The officer's report noted he was spitting, angry, embittered and he 'was going to kill the bitch' as soon as he got out.

In those three days, I filed for an injunction. I was granted an early court date based on the severity of the situation.

I wasn't there the first time he appeared in court because I had been advised to not be there.

I was unprepared for the resulting legal chaos coming down the road. Due to the intense emotional and physical abuse, I was worn out. I had no reservoirs of strength to look to in this time of need. I needed to regroup and re-strengthen myself, but I didn't have the time to do so. I had to figure out a way I was going to survive the next few months.

After three days of being locked up, *he* had reached his boiling point. I had spent three days of being away from work. I found myself in a frozen mental state. I couldn't think or process what was going on around me. I came to the point where I recognized my life, as I knew it was totally over. The emotional mechanisms within me that were designed to bring about my restoration were no longer functioning.

I knew I had to redesign myself. Through this process, I became intimately familiar with the criminal justice system and how it worked. Much to my dismay, I learned being the victim doesn't guarantee you success in the courts. Just as everything else in life, it was a game. *He,* being the master chameleon at the art of schizophrenia, knew how to play the game as a professional.

He chose to disobey the injunction that had been granted. As soon as he posted bail, even though the courts told him a condition of his bail was for him to stay away from the house, he still decided he was the ruler of me. As such, he embarked on a campaign to undermine my fragile emotional stability.

He violated his bail by driving within 500 feet of the house. He would park at the end of the block (which wasn't but two houses away from ours) and call the house as often as he could. At first, I would receive phone calls that detailed specific threats from him to me. Then I would get hang-ups. I had the neighbors on lookout for him; they would telephone the police as soon as they saw him. That wasn't enough to keep him away.

One morning, as I was walking through the house, I saw him outside the window, looking at me. By the time I screamed and ran to phone the police, he had already disappeared. He had appeared before the judge so many times for violating his bail the judge had to threaten to lock him up again. He didn't care. His campaign was to get me broken down and he was relentless in his pursuit of that goal.

I, on the other hand, tried to go back to work. But because I had been so emotionally broken, I couldn't really confront work. So I obtained doctor's notes to confirm my absences. I finally called one day to tell them I was willing to return to work. What they did was ask me to go for an interview with the manager to determine my work-worthiness. On my return, I found out my supervisor had been let go as well as the Human Resources manager. I was now placed in front of a new manager who had no familiarity with me and who thought I was quite disposable.

The week before Thanksgiving, the new manager thanked me for the time I had given the company and told me to file for unemployment. I had been away from work for three weeks, which, in any other case, was grounds for dismissal; but I had specific doctor's orders to not go anywhere near the workplace.

To make matters worse, it was a man who told me. Now, a man had viciously physically and emotionally abused me. Then I went before another wicked man who was a legal authority who denied me the ability to permanently stabilize myself as a citizen of the country. And now, here I was before another man, who told me that I was now out of a job. Now what was I going to do? I had a mortgage to pay, a child to feed; I had myself to sustain? How was I going to do that if I didn't have a job?

I drove back home and sat down. I was too weak to cry. I curled up on the sofa, then called my therapist, and confided in her that I didn't think I was ever going to get out of this.

In an effort to stave off depression, she called me in for further counseling. She explained to mc the process I was going through. She informed me unemployment provided some form of sustenance that would sustain my daughter and I for a while, and it was better than nothing. In the meantime, I was to find an attorney because I would need one in coming divorce proceedings.

That was another thing: I had finally decided to file for divorce. I had gone to court and filed *pro se* as an indigent, meaning I was filing for myself on my own behalf without having any means of paying for it. I submitted the documents to court and that was how Sam learned he was getting divorced.

Once that process started, I began to go about rebuilding my life. Even though I would have to go to court to face *him*, there was the matter of our daughter. Her place in my life was such that I was willing to fight for her as long as it meant I would keep her. *He*, on the other hand, had a plan to prove me an unfit mother. He filed for sole custody of her on those grounds. He also claimed because I wasn't a landed resident, I had no permanency in the country and was therefore unable to take care of her. That was the bane of his argument.

We were sent to family court to resolve the matter. In family court, you were sent to arbitration in an effort to resolve the matter in a peaceable way. The person who sits over the arbitration isn't called a judge, but a general master. That person is an attorney who is also a judge. When we went to arbitration, there were two cases pending. One case was the criminal case of assault and battery he perpetrated on my person; then there was the divorce proceeding with resulting family separation and child custody issues. Make no doubt about it: he intended to win it all.

He had forgotten the tiger that awakened in me. He hadn't encountered that tiger in a while, and he had yet to deal with me.

The first injunction of protection was only temporary and it expired shortly. So I went to file for a permanent one. I was then placed before a female judge. When I walked into the courtroom for my case to be heard, I noticed there were mostly women in there. Every person who filed for an injunction was denied one, especially if they were female. I, too, was denied. But I couldn't understand why because the judge was a woman. I was reeling from shock. How was I going to survive if I didn't have an injunction against him?

So I re-filed. A second time, the injunction was again cast down. I sat in the same courtroom before the same female judge and thought *something must be wrong*. The third try, I was sitting in the back of the courtroom thinking the same thing. I got up and I walked downstairs to file again. As I did, I met a guy who introduced himself as an attorney and gave me his card.

Why does this judge seem to have a problem with females? She appeared to have a greater perpetuity to deny injunctions filed by women, especially when children were involved. It seemed uncanny those were the cases she specifically denied the most.

I ran into the guy who had introduced himself as an attorney.

"I heard you mumbling to yourself in the courtroom back there," he said. "There's a story behind that judge."

"No kidding," I said.

Then he went on to explain she had a personal vendetta against women because her current husband had been denied visitation rights by his previous wife to see his daughter. It wasn't until the daughter had grown up considerably that she could see him. And so, because of this, this particular female judge had a vendetta against all women, specifically women who had children, because she herself couldn't have children. She felt she had been denied that opportunity because of her husband's previous wife.

"You've got to be kidding me," I said, astounded.

Once I found that out, I marched to my attorney's office, and I told her if they didn't find out what was wrong with that judge, I was going to take it to the news. They didn't believe me. So I walked up to a news reporter who was standing on the steps of the court house covering another case, and I told him my name and my story; how I'd been denied an injunction from an abusive man three times by the same judge each time. I walked back into my attorney's office only to be admonished by her.

"You can't do that!"

"Why not? She can deny me an injunction three times for no apparent reason and I can't go to the news about it?"

"But she's a judge and she's very powerful."

"I could care less about her worthless power. I'm a poor person, I'm female and my back is up against the wall. And this woman is using her personal feelings to refuse me from protection from a wicked man who has beaten me over and over and over again. I'm not about to sit back and take that!"

The reporter started making phone calls to investigate the story. Before I knew it, on the fourth try, my injunction was granted. The minute it was granted, if he so much as showed up within a few feet of the house, the police would be called. He had already gone back to jail twice for violating the terms of his bail, but after the second time, he decided it was better to stay away. That was good news for me.

The criminal case against him was in process. I still had to face the civil case, which was the matter of custody. He fought and obtained an attorney who was a misogynist (a man who, despite not being homosexual, hated women). This attorney decided he was going to make sure I would never stand a chance.

When we went to court for the trial of the criminal case, it was a trial by jury. His attorney, as representative of a jury of his peers, had selected the jury. I was shocked at how he showed up in court; he was dressed in his suit and tie, looking like an innocent choirboy. I was dressed in a suit as well.

His attorney painted him to be a caring citizen and painted me out to be a scoundrel. Despite this stage of lies, the attorney was inept, unprofessional and unprepared. But that didn't seem to be a problem for the judge, who, as he watched the attorney stumble through the ordinance that governed the matter, helped the attorney along.

When I was placed on the witness stand, he tried to object to something. The judge asked him on what grounds. He couldn't correctly state the statute he was citing. The judge even asked him "Did you mean…"

I turned to the judge and said, "Your honor, you are supposed to be impartial. You are helping the attorney against me. You're not supposed to be helping him to remember; that's his job. You're supposed to be the judge who is to decide the matter fairly. I feel now I will never get a fair trial in this courtroom. I have to file a complaint." Despite everyone's shocked faces, I continued.

"Is this the old boy's club again? Is it because he's a lawyer and you're a judge and you're both men you all decide to gang up against the victim? Not only have I been victimized by this man, I'm being victimized in a court of law where I'm supposed to receive a fair, impartial hearing."

After a stunned silence, the judge turned to the prosecutor and said, "She doesn't need you to defend her. She's defending herself."

The judge ended up recusing himself from the case. The jury, however, came back and found *Sam* not guilty. He didn't serve any time because they felt he served enough time, and that was the end of that.

That little incident made *his* attorney see red; he was so mad. But he still knew the one area he could hurt me the most was in the custody of my daughter.

In the custody case, I was beyond shock when *his* attorney had the nerve to stand up in that courtroom and accuse me of being a woman of the streets.

"Isn't it true that you were a prostitute in your native country when my client met you?" he boldly asked me when I was on the witness stand.

"That's a lie," I said. Then I turned to *Sam* and said, "How could you tell such a blatant lie?"

I looked at the judge and said, "Are you going to let this carry on? This man is maligning me in public and telling brazen lies on me?"

When Sam and I met I had been working as an Administrative Assistant in a large chemical Company, which had their regional offices in my hometown. In addition to which I had attended Community College, graduated high school, entered two beauty pageants, modeled and had a career in Public Relations and Insurance. By the end of the marriage, mine was the only income, and I provided health insurance and transportation in addition to paying the housekeeper, the handyman, utilities, food clothing etc. In my recollection, he never paid for anything for Alex. In fact it was the toughest time emotionally for me as a young mother and wife to discover the man I had married was derelict in his duties as a provider. Imagine my consternation thirteen years later to be placed on the witness stand and be called a whore? Are you kidding me as I look back over all the times I had to take Alex to the doctor, had to borrow a friend's car when I didn't have one, used a company car to run personal errands, because he didn't provide one? Sam knew the truth and chose to ignore it at my expense, because the people sitting in the courtroom wouldn't have known. What they saw was a young woman, whom they believed could move on with her life. They wouldn't see the destruction Sam brought to my life.

Justice. What justice? I found no justice in that courtroom. I hoped if I lost on the assault charges, I would win in family court. My goodness, I needed more than hope to survive this round.

You see it is not enough for the abuser to destroy another person physically and emotionally. There are other ways they choose to abuse. In my experiences with the justice system, I was often shocked at the ways in which abusive men, who sometimes through their own cunning and planning, and strategizing, often secure better attorneys simply because they can pay more. Too often, they walk away a winner in these cases. Something has got to give. We cannot continue to allow them to win by beating a woman and winning primary custody while winning against her through the system. Somehow, we have to develop ways to afford women in abusive situations financial aid so they can have better representation in the courts.

15
Things You Should Know

I want to point out; an abusive man is a clever man. He has designed a system of entrapment to cause a woman to fall. From day one, he has already foreseen a day in court; while you are busy feeling you are in love, he is already planning your complete destruction. He will make sure not only will he have his day in court, but also he will win.

Hence the reason for a part of his plan to ruin you; not only will he permanently destroy you physically, and batter you emotionally, but he will completely decimate you by removing your children, demonstrating and perpetuating same behavior patterns to cause them to be abusers. And like an evil conniving devil, he sits back to watch as you go through hoops to try to stop his plans. He never intended for you to win. At the same time, he knows you, and he knows the one thing you want to do is remove your children from him having any type of emotional influence on them. He knows you know if he gets a chance, he can ruin those children and, in so doing, ruin you at the same time.

Keep in mind you are not dealing with a Mr. Nice Guy. There is no nice guy here, nothing but a man who intends to completely and utterly destroy you. Sam wanted to get back at me because it was my reputation that had given me good jobs back home. Those good jobs provided him with comfort so now he was tearing me down. I just felt this was his way of getting back at me. He was a psychopath because he enjoyed watching me become uncomfortable. Just as he had enjoyed watching my face crumple when he slapped me.

But he did take the judge seriously when the judge warned him the last time; the judge said if he were to appear in that courtroom again in that county for harassing and hitting me, he would be sent to jail for life. Now that he couldn't hit me anymore, he used his lies and his words to hit me. I felt as if I were being raped all over again. This time I was raped in a court of law for all to see.

Now it was time for arbitration in the custody battle. At this time, I was forced to call character witnesses for myself. The only people *he* and I had in common, who knew us from when we began, and who knew anything about my background, were my family. So I called my mother and my sister, who flew to Orlando, to attend court as character witnesses for me.

When they arrived, this brought forth a whole different view of the matter. Once they gave their testimony, all the things Sam had accused me of doing (being a whore and being an unfit mother) were thrown through the window. He tried a malicious undermining of me in the eyes of the court by declaring me an unfit mother when there was nothing substantiating that claim. Mom was livid. "How could you say those things about my daughter?" she asked him in front of the judge. You knew who she was when you met her. You were nobody, I told my daughter not to marry you for I could see this would happen, to her if she did, and I am proven right". I'm glad you are out of her life, you were not good enough for her" And that was that. The Judge looked at him and his attorney as if they were the scum of the earth. Boy, did vindication feel well. After all I had been through, someone finally stood up to him and defended me and my honor in a court of law. This was good.

My therapist sometimes came to court with me because the situation was so emotionally traumatic. I got to see, firsthand, what abusive men do to women who try to leave them alive. This forms part of the pattern of destruction abusers weave once a victim becomes entangled in the web. It is normal for abusers to accuse the victim of being unfit to do anything.

Can you imagine being declared an unfit mother when you were the one who had to protect yourself and your child from the emotional and physical violence someone wreaks in your life?

Unbelievable. When all you've ever done for your child is to love, protect and provide for her? I remember many days when *he* was absent emotionally from her life, because he was too busy physically wreaking havoc in my life by beating me in front of the same child of whom he was trying to get custody. Sam engaged in physical battering of my person; so how did I end up being the 'unfit parent'?

The first attorney I hired was drunk and fell asleep, literally and figuratively on the case. But, luckily for me she had a partner who asked her to step aside because she was ruining it for me. My new attorney was as sharp as a two-edged sword. She wasted no time in filing motions to have Sam's ridiculous motions dismissed; and my new attorney requested my mother and sister act as character witnesses, defending me.

It was late 2001 by this time, and the case seemed to be dragging on and on and on. Isn't it amazing at the end of it all, he was the one hanging on? The reality is an abuser likes to be in control and nothing satisfied Sam more than knowing that due to his actions or inactions he somehow manages to exert control over the course of my everyday life. An abuser seems to enjoy some kind of vicarious pleasure in watching the family endure hardships inflicted on the victim. I remember many days going to court to have the case postponed for no reason than *he* seemed not to want me to get on with my life.

And this is why I recommend therapy because in my case, it proved insightful and became a guide to helping me watch for these kinds of situations so I could develop a thick skin. This insight enabled me to survive protracted emotional abuse. For surely it was continued emotional abuse to be dragged into court at Sam's whim and fancy as he and his attorney dreamt up one silly thing after another.

Because the justice system is designed to give everyone a fair say, he had no intention of letting me get away without some further damage to my emotional psyche. He had no intention of letting me develop a life consisting of a healthy emotional relationship with any man. What the abusive man intends to do is determine complete emotional devastation to his prey, rendering her incapable of making any kind of sustainable emotion decisions in the future. After leaving an abuser, at some point, the victim will likely come back to the abuser, and this is where the victim would be crazy to think of ever being alone again with the abuser in any kind of relationship.

He will be so nice and ply you with charm and kisses, hang the sun, moon, and stars with his hands in your favor, and then the next time, we will be singing nearer my God to thee at your funeral.

The next set of flowers you will receive will be ones placed on your coffin. For the abusive man, if he gets a chance to have you once more in his grasp, has no intention of letting you get away from him again.

He will cut off all connections with you and the outside world. Many times you have heard, in these situations, of him suddenly changing jobs and moving out of state, leaving town, and taking you and the children. And he uses as a guise, *I want my family to stay together*. If you stay with him long enough to hear these words, you should run for your life. He has no intention of letting you get away, but in fact has a plan to keep you trapped. And if you are alienated and isolated from friends and family, as was issue in my case, you feel you have no one to go to.

He will make sure you understand, as he will tell it to you over and over again. The he begins to cut off your connections with new found friends in the new town you have begun this new life in. He will make it difficult for you to keep a job as you saw in my story, where he would show up at work and make a scene for your employer to fire you. Then he will engage in a pattern of intense physical violence, making sure you cannot go to work with black and blue marks, and bruises.

He will also make sure he demeans you enough that you remain emotionally sensitive and cannot accept reprimand or correction from any male authority figure. And as most of us report to a male boss, you can imagine how sensitive you appear to be when, for example, he says *Sue, you need to type this over, what were you thinking?* Then you burst into tears and he says *what's the matter? You can't take a little correction?* Your male boss begins to think you have a problem in competence and accepting direction. When in fact his tone of voice reminds you of what you endure at home daily.

It seems to me that most abusive men lack formal education. By that I mean they have never studied for any program requiring dedication and discipline. But he can be one smart dude. In fact many of them work dead end jobs or jobs requiring little or no skill. Yet these are the same individuals with the most success in destroying many women financially, emotionally and physically.

Many women, including the professionally successful ones, have fallen victims to an abusive man's seductive charms. Be careful for his is a carefully constructed web of deceit, which he created to hide his destructive motives. So many women have been fooled into believing the lies they have been told by men of this personality.

That is not to suggest that educated and professional men are not abusers. Violence, in my experience, is a learned behavior. What causes a man who has enjoyed admiration of his peers, a degree of professional success and community respect to share the same courtroom, or prison cell, with a man who has not had the benefit of his formal training and education?

Somewhere in his past, he learned this is the way to treat women in his life and who become members of his family. Somewhere he learned in order to exert some amount of control over his life, he has to maintain control by all means necessary, and he has designed a program specifically aimed at using and employing his methods of control.

It doesn't matter who he is. If he is the CEO of multinational corporation, a respected judge, President of the Rotary Club, politician who has risen to the pinnacle and corridors of power, one thing I know is somewhere in his past, he learned violence as a means of control to get from women what he wants. It is the same profile that fits rapists. Just as rape is about sex, dominion and power, in the same way violence in the home is about sex, dominion and power.

I lived through too many accusations of having sex with other men to know how preoccupied a violent man is about sex. I came away from that experience wondering when would he realize my feelings of sexual attraction had been killed by his emotional abuse. A woman and her emotions towards her partner cannot be divorced. Hence the reason if a man is hitting her, emotionally abusing her, or forced her to have an abortion because he doesn't want any more children, she cannot have feelings of intimacy towards him. There is no sexual gratification for the woman. Some of you have experienced a tightening in areas where you should be experiencing release and cannot achieve any level of orgasms.

To her, he represents the person who defiled her and reduced her self worth. And because her self worth is tied up in how she feels, she just can't be sexually attracted to him or feel any desire. Most women who have been through some kind of abuse need therapy in order to have normal relations with men. I strongly recommend therapy. In my experience, all men are not bad. Just a few who seem to treat women as if they are an extension of themselves and have no other reason for existence except to serve as personal battering rams. And he practices his beliefs with a degree of sophisticated precision and planning.

For this individual to remain undetected by his fellow professionals, and colleagues, he undergoes a double side life, one in which no one outside the members of his household would ever guess his wife is on the receiving end of the brunt of his fists.

Many of you who are reading this today have either experienced this or know someone who has experienced abuse. But in an effort to retain your comfortable lifestyle, you continue to place yourselves in danger of becoming a victim of domestic violence. You choose to gamble your life on what are material possessions and social status. How many more excuses do you need before you fall down the stairs again? Do you figure the next time, you just might break your neck. If this sounds harsh to you, let this be your wake-up call; violence against women and children exists on every level in society.

In fact many of you wouldn't let your friends know you are reading this book. You would be too ashamed to have anyone know you have been victimized and battered at the hands of your successful and respected spouse. As unbelievable as it is, you realize now there is no difference between your white-collar husband and the guy who ends up on the six o'clock news, handcuffed and looking like he is in need of a good grooming. You have felt first-hand the effects of your own husband's well-manicured hands and his many punches to your stomach. You have seen the cultured veneer slide right off his face and become nothing but the sneer of an evil man with no moral character, a boy who wants his own power trip.

Many of these men are victims as well. They stood by and watched helplessly as their fathers abused their mothers, sisters, cousins or someone with whom they are related. It is totally unbelievable how the prison system is filled with sons of women who had to step in to defend their mothers from men who were connected to them through some family type relationship. In our society, violence carries a social stigma that it only happens to people who are in a certain socio-economic class.

Do you want to hear about my well-traveled husband who drank cognacs before dinner and who wore French cuff shirts? Do you want to hear about the swimming pool and tennis court in my backyard? Would you believe that he hit me when the housekeeper was off? Can you identify with Sam who wore dress shirts and whose pocket squares matched his ties. I used to fear that his monogrammed silverware would end up in my throat one day. Be not fooled by the veneers these sociopath individuals wear to disguise and fool you into thinking they are normal and upstanding law-abiding citizens. You are reading the story of a man who named amongst his friends the local police chief, politicians, and community leaders.

You have even learned how to cover it up by excusing away bruises by saying you fell down the stairs, canceling appointments due to not feeling well, not going to certain places, describing it as a conflict in scheduling. You know your husband as clever as he is, knows women like me who have survived and won't let you have friends who can readily identify his character traits. In fact when you meet new friends, he chooses them for you and tells you which ones to keep. They have to meet his approval before you can socialize with them. He chooses which charities you back and support, which friends you associate with it, what functions and events you go to, what you wear, where you lunch, what car you drive; he even checks at the end of the day how many miles you have driven by reading your car's odometer. And you excuse it all away by declaring he cares about me and is just careful of what I do.

When are you going to wake up and see it for what it is? Domestic abuse knows no boundaries. Just like any disease, it crosses all racial, ethnic, and social lines. I discovered some commonalities as I journeyed from 'battered in my home' to being 'battered in court'. This world is still an old boys network. You will find there are only a few individuals who, despite being male, will rise to your defense and support you.

It is easier said than done that justice is fair. Take no chances with the justice system but arm and equip yourself for the fight of your life. You cannot afford to sit back and think the system will defend you. No. The system is designed to benefit the person who can execute the best performance in court in front of the jury and judge. Your abusive spouse or partner will walk away with the Best Actor award. Every abusive man knows this. Why are you shocked at the well-groomed, clean-shaven, man who shows up for his hearing?

You are left in the dust wearing the signs of emotional and physical abuse you went through. Now, with whom do you think the jury will side?

You need to have the mindset of a General marching into war. This is what this is: your partner had designed and set this up long before he met you and intended to destroy you from the day you met. He had a carefully constructed plan to see to your immediate and total destruction. You have to be careful you are not left on the sidelines watching events unfold around you in court as if you were a bystander in your own life.

Every nuance of your character and personality will be made out to seem as if you were a person undeserving of breathing air on the planet. Despite your accomplishments and many achievements, you will sound as if your life is worth nothing and the old boys network is hard at work, making sure you appear to be the one with the problem. The perception is whatever a woman says about how her husband treats her is nothing but idle chatter. The boys will engage in a program of ridicule to make it seem as if this nice man, who is dressed up, is a decent man who works to provide for his family. If he enjoys some latitude and profile in the community, he will be declared a pillar of society.

Sounds horrific? You bet it is. For all the advances women have made, professionally and socially, and for all the men who have helped us to move forward in fields that previously were occupied by men, women, by and large, are still seen as commodities to be traded by men. I have encountered differing attitudes amid professional men. I have listened to their conversations and ways in which they excuse their emotional cruelty towards their wives.

Abusers have become absolutely adept at circumventing the system in order to achieve what they desire, which is not to spend a night in jail. Sam used to tell me he would hit me in soft places. I am now quite familiar with the feel of having the wind knocked out of me as his fists punched me in the abdomen.

As women we need to pay attention to what a man does before we get married and we need to learn to discern, through his speech, thoughts, mannerisms and observations, his likely foretold patterns of behavior. My therapist used to say a man tell us his plans, but we are so in love with the idea of being in love we do not listen clearly. In his attitudes and mannerisms are his intentions. And that is why you have to be surrounded by friends and family when dating so they can see what you cannot.

It is not a coincidence he tries to remove you from influence of family and friends. He knows exactly what he is doing. Abusive men are extremely clever, and they have developed a deceptive system of charm and seduction, which is sociopathic in its profile. He becomes whatever you need him to be. This pattern lasts three to six months. He can only sustain his nice guy image for that long, as after a while, his thin veneer of deception wears completely off and he stands as the naked abuser he is.

We need to tune in to things a man says. As soon as he starts complaining about your friends, glancing at your cell phone when it rings, calling you frequently, it is time for you to move on. Dismiss him and remove him totally from your life. These behaviors we have just identified are the platform for ultimate control mechanisms he will unleash on you as the relationship progresses. Too many women, who have experienced this behavior, tell themselves, *oh he cares about me*.

The women perceive *his* methods of control as caring. In many cases, some women feel this way due to a lack of understanding of roles played by men in their lives. All too often, Daddy is absent thereby creating a vacuum for someone else to step in and fill the gap.

A woman who has had no fatherly contact is not aware a part of her emotional desire for her man is to make up for what Daddy didn't do. So in an effort to be whole, she looks for love in the wrong place. And this is just the design into which an abuser walks. He knows this; in fact many abusers prey on women with these particular sets of experiences.

Abusers know who to go after and what tools to apply to turn a situation in their favor, and they believe they are adept and skilled at it. Then you have women who have had fathers but their fathers were abusive to their mothers, and for some reason, they haven't analyzed, they seem to be attracted to men who are controlling.

But initially it's not about control; they seem to get along with men who are the strong type. This is just a hidden way of saying he will eventually cut off all your life support systems from around you and leave you completely dependent on him. And there are women who were raised in, what appeared to be, perfectly balanced homes, but who were pushed into marriages with men whose emotional issues were hidden beneath a veneer of success.

His success was that he is a CEO, Doctor, lawyer, politician, entrepreneur; he certainly plays the role of the 'successful man about town' image. Because that's all it is, an image, a thin veneer that shuts off when he gets home and drives into the garage.

How many of you know the sound of that garage door closing as if it is the sound of the nail driving into your coffin. I wonder, amongst your friends and co-workers, which one of you is dreading going home this evening, knowing the inevitable questioning and interrogation will lead to pushing and shoving.

Don't be jealous of the woman you see at the Mall, buying high-end purses, jewelry and other items. You might be surprised to know the price she will pay later for her purchases. Don't envy anyone's life for you don't know at what cost he or she has earned it. We need to learn to be less jealous of one another and find ways in which we can cooperate and help one another effectively battle emotional and physical violence.

Some women are not abused at their homes. They are abused at work. There are men who feel it is their God given duty to force themselves on women whom they supervise. It seems they enjoy the power trip that comes with their position as they subject women in their employment to sexual and emotional abuse, often leaving women to file a complaint, or in many cases, deal with it because they need the job.

These men are predators who prey on a woman's vulnerabilities, whether they are economic or professional. An abuser will use his power to obtain what he wants, the thrill of knowing he is in supreme control of his women subjects and this is a dilemma for many as you face economic deprivation if you don't work.

Sometimes this is the only position or job available, or you need to keep this job because you have a sick spouse or sick child, or house payments, or child in college. Due to these extenuating circumstances, many women choose to endure abusive behavior and develop coping mechanisms rather than report incidents.

Too many women have sat in their cars in the parking lots of office buildings and outside their homes crying at the level of abuse and emotional depravity, and sometimes even physical, as they had to give up their bodies in order to keep a job. This is why we need better legislation to protect women from these situations. Sexual harassment laws have done much to reduce instances, but law hasn't gone far enough in apprehending men who find a way to operate within loopholes. Somehow, there is enough justification on their part to continue foraging a way to exact emotional and physical damage to a woman's career and her sustainable economic growth.

As women, we have to find ways to support one another and if you are in a position of power and are reading this, you can make a difference. By ensuring this behavior is not a part of your organization, you have done enough for your employees to talk about the kind of acceptable patterns of behavior you practice. This will go a long way as in today's world, women blog and read other women's blogs about issues that concern us.

So as we continue to stand for one another, more and more women will become aware of legislation already existing that protects them. And for many of you out there, the next time you see a woman sitting in front of you who has come to your agency seeking shelter, food or some assistance due to violent physical and emotional situation in her home, don't stand in her way. Provide her with as much help as you can to let her know of other community resources she can take advantage of. And when we see each other in the Malls, and shopping centers, grocery stores, schools, PTA, soccer practice, piano and dancing lessons, let us learn to smile with one another and see in what ways we can help one another. It starts with just one.

16

Closure

Our house eventually went into foreclosure and I had known it would only be a matter of time before this happened. During this upheaval, I sent my daughter, Alex to be with my mother and my sister in Detroit, to give her some time to be away from emotional turmoil. I had to find somewhere else to live and did not want her to be exposed to the uncertainties and displacement that ensued. I had tried to negotiate with Sam to sell the house, prior to the bank filing foreclosure proceedings. The agreement I had negotiated with the bank was to sell the house so that we could walk away with some cash on hand. We would have each walked away with approximately $60,000.

However, on the advice of his attorney, Sam chose not to sign the sale agreement. He later told me how much he regretted that decision. What would make a man so consumed by his purposeful destruction of my life to consciously deny making money?

It seemed as if abuse was not enough. I felt as though I were losing my mind. Everywhere I turned, something was hammered at me. First, it was *him* beating me up. Then, it was immigration authorities denying me based on a letter of lies *he* wrote. Then, I was fired from my job. Next, it was the judge who refused to grant me an injunction until I complained. Then, I was being raped over in the court by a judge who was trying to diminish the fact this man had beaten me several times.

At one point, I had to remind *his* lawyer that my character wasn't on trial. What was on trial was the fact his client hit me over and over again. The attorney wasn't supposed to be calling my character into witness. Neither my character nor background have anything to do with the fact in our home, Sam stood up, whipped, slapped, kicked and beat me up until the night when the sheriff's deputies came to the house.

Here I was again, becoming subject to another man's dominion. It seemed to me I was surrounded by domineering men. It was at that time I determined somehow, when I got out of this, I was going to become a voice for those women who had no power. As disenfranchised and dispossessed as I was, I determined this too was going to pass. When it did, I was going to make sure I had enough power and money to help other women who have gone through things like this.

When we went to Arbitration to petition for custody, he again brought up the 'unfit mother by way of whoredom' claim. It was my own mother who challenged him. She said, "Let me remind you of something. I was there when you married my daughter. Do you remember? I was there when my granddaughter was born. In fact, I remember being there when you weren't there. So how dare you accuse my daughter of being a whore? I worked, sent her to school and raised her to be a young lady. How *dare* you accuse her of being a whore! Just because she's here at your mercy, you feel you can walk over her? And now you want to take her daughter away from her? You have a pattern of abusing women in your life and getting away with it. Now you want to do it to my daughter? How dare you!"

It was the weight of my family's testimony that caused the judge to look at the situation fairly. This new general master was able to say something had gone terribly wrong. When *his* attorney accused me of being a whore and called me a liar, as far as I was concerned, he was just driving more nails into his coffin. Not only were those vicious lies; even if his client told him that, he, as an attorney, should not have presented evidence in a court of law without backing it up with the facts. If he knew it wasn't true, he had done me just as wrong as *Sam* had.

I was still walking through the fire, but the intensity had dramatically died down. Even if the temperature didn't decrease, I wasn't going to be burned because it wasn't my *destiny* to be burned. Whenever we went to court, he always brought up the same thing. It almost became too much. So I decided to do something about it.

I wrote to the Bar Association where we lived and filed a complaint against his attorney. I detailed how he had called me names in court that he was unable to back up with evidence. I spoke of how his questioning of me on the stand was unjust, impersonal and injurious; the language he used to speak with me was filled with personal contempt, not professional impartialness.

The Bar communicated to me they would investigate my claims. I later learned they had done a thorough investigation and when the investigation was complete, they found he was in violation of the ethical standards of his profession. He was disciplined for it; he was placed on probation. By the time the full-scale investigation was over, he had been stripped of his license. I later found out Sam could not have chosen a better man for the job. His attorney was a misogynist and his hatred of women was manifested in his spurious comments about women personally. I kept wondering it was rather unusual for an attorney to pursue the plaintiff as he did me. There was something about his attack bordering on personal distaste. I had enough experience around criminal lawyers to know they handle cases with some emotional detachment. But in this case, it was too familiar. He seemed to enjoy hurting me for the sheer pleasure of it. And I had enough of being used by Sam and any man whom he chose to represent him.

Here's the case: in a typical abusive divorce proceeding, your demented spouse will find the cruelest attorney he can find. This was true in my case. Not only did this guy hate me for being against his client, but also he hated me for being female. You have to prepare yourself for the battle that lies ahead. Words cannot prepare you for the carnage you will go through in court. Some days you will feel so drained, that you will wish the end would come sooner than later. And your former spouse will just seem to be getting better and better. See, he has been well prepared for this, emotionally, more than you have been. You didn't see him as the train wreck that was coming to hit your life. It's like a game of chess you move, he moves, then checkmate.

For me, time was slowly marching on; it was now November of 2001. Towards the end of the summer, we had agreed to a settlement, which would entail *Sam* having partial visitation rights. The agreement outlined his visitation rights to have Alex every other weekend. There were strict guidelines dictating the manner in which pick-ups and drop-offs would be conducted. In spite of this he continued with his emotional battering, but I had learned to tune him out as his time in my life was coming to an end.

I had other issues to deal with.

Whenever Alex was with him, you would think he would try to spend time with her to reassure her and make her feel better. Nope.

Instead he kept telling her how wicked and evil her mother was and how her mother took everything from him and on and on. The poor child would beg me to not go to his house. She would tell me how he spent the whole weekend talking about me. But there was nothing I could do about it because it was court-ordered. If I violated it, I could risk losing permanent custody of my child. All I could do was comfort her and promise her she wouldn't have to deal with this one day. The emotional abuse continued, even to Alex, as he used her to send messages to me knowing full well how distressed I would be at the continued abuse he was exposing to her. This is why, as women, we have to be careful about the men we choose to settle with. Because once you have children, you are tied to him for the rest of your life. Even when you divorce, you have to attend school outings, birthdays, graduations, eventually weddings, and hospital stays to watch the next generation appear in life. The point is, choose wisely and you will save yourself a ton of trouble. When we create children with someone, we have effectively tied our life and our soul with that person. If you don't know their value systems and if the values turn out to not coincide with yours, you have just about initiated a battle royal to see who is the most influential with the child.

The abuser intends to alienate and isolate you from your children. It is part of the emotional and mental terror he plans to unleash in your life. You will eventually begin to think you are living with a terrorist who intends to cause as much collateral damage as he can, while he can, and disable you from recovery. The best I can tell you is watch out. At the end of this book, I have created a list of personality traits to watch out for. Use them and get to be intimately familiar. The list will guide you in making choices fundamentally affecting your life.

Later on in that year, *Sam* decided to call for a settlement out of nowhere. He announced he was moving back to New York, where it had all began for him. A place where he was comfortable and surrounded by his buddies, and because he was moving, he suggested we finalize the custody agreement. He finally agreed Alex was better off with me. The morning he was scheduled to get on the plane and leave for New York, he called and apologized to Alex and to me. I couldn't believe it. He apologized for all the hell he had taken us through, for being emotionally abusive when I had moved on with my life. He even asked for my forgiveness and wished me all the best. Imagine that. Wishes for all the best? Really?

Then, he got on the plane and it was over.

Not once during the process did he ever pay child support. He never contributed one dollar to purchasing anything for her, never asked where did money come from to provide for her basic needs. He did agree to pay child support, but that was short-lived because before the ink was dried on the agreement, he left town, which rendered that agreement null and void as he had left the jurisdiction of the court. Wow, was all I could say. But that was okay, for I now had my life back. I was now free to think and be I. I was finally able to play and hug Alex and take her on long walks, and trips to the Mall, and day trips to Disney and all the theme parks in the area.

I was now finally able to exhale. *So that's why he moved*, I thought. *Sly.* He made sure of that. I later learned child support does not raise children. It provides for them financially and communicates to them that *Daddy cares about me enough to want to make sure that I am fed and live in a safe, comfortable environment.* But essentially when a man leaves a woman, the subliminal message he communicates to the child is *I left you too. I don't care about you.* And men become so caught up in their passionate abuse of the woman, they don't see the effects on children. Guys, there are never any excuses not to call your children, visit them, love them, email, text, write, send a message from space. They need to be assured even if you and Mommy can't live together, *I love you and it has nothing to do with you*. I can't begin to tell you how many children I know of who, at some point, blame themselves for their parents' separation.

I know we as parents made a mistake having children when we got together, as time proved we could not live together. But we need to find a way for the children's sake to cultivate an atmosphere of co-existence, just for their peace of mind. And stop the fighting. Stop trying to control events in your ex-wife's household, stop thinking you are still her spouse and can tell her what to do. Learn to make peace with the debacle you have created. And stay in touch for the emotional well being of your children. Enough said.

My old friend, Kathy at the finance company who helped me to consolidate my debt, had been right about Sam in every aspect.

His moving was the best Thanksgiving present I could ever receive. He had moved over a thousand miles away and he had taken all the pressure, anxiety and turmoil with him.

He was gone.

I was giddy with happiness. But we still weren't officially divorced yet. I couldn't figure out why he was still clinging on to something that wasn't even real.

Finally, in March of 2002, my divorce was officially granted. What began in October 2000 took him two years to finally realize his reign of terror had ended.

I can't forget walking into the courtroom. As I stood in front of the same judge who refused to grant my injunction three times, I now realized this nightmare had run its course. The saying proves true, eventually all things do work together for our good. This was the same judge who had presided over the divorce proceedings. I requested my maiden name be restored; she granted my request and wished me the best in all my future endeavors. Then she smiled.

As we walked out of the courtroom and stood on the courthouse steps, I extended my hand to *his* and said, "This is it. It's *over*." Imagine that what once began as a love story was now ending with a handshake.

I was stunned as he turned to me and said "Oh my God. I just lost my best friend."

"Which friend is that?" I too was startled.

His next words were truly surprising.

He chuckled and said "You. You were my best friend all these years. I now realize that you were my best friend. And I've lost you."

More like I was your punching bag all these years. But it's ok because it's over now.

"That's too bad," I said shaking my head. "That's just too bad."

Epilogue

In the years since my divorce from Sam, I have written and published two books, *Visions* in 2004 and more recently *Musings of the Spirit*. *Through The Fire* is my third book. Some parts of this book were written while I was experiencing the incidents described in this volume. Thank you for taking the time out to read this book. You have truly blessed me by buying and reading the stories I have written. I consider myself blessed to have survived domestic violence. I encourage you to donate to charities in your area and support initiatives of various community groups who provide much needed support to my sisters and friends who have been victims of violence. Please consider donating today and know you are changing someone's life.

Alex is now off to college and intends to pursue a law degree. Her dream is to one day be able to help women who are going though divorce and whose lives have been affected by domestic violence. I intend to give her my fullest support.

harrietcammock.org

My Top Fifty List

1. Jealousy and possessiveness.
2. Seductive qualities *(not like Clark Gable, but in the Braveheart kind of way, if you get my meaning).*
3. Too much Charisma (take note of capital 'C').
4. Seems to be the answer to your dreams *(if he seems to be too good to be true, he is).*
5. The feeling of being swept off your feet (see next).
6. Whirlwind courtship *(it's not as romantic as it sounds).*
7. Pressures you to commit early in relationship, before you've had a chance to 'feel it out'.
8. Control *(this by itself is an entirely new subject that will eventually have its own list.)* Think: manipulation and feelings of superiority to the female race.
9. Monitor and eavesdrop on your conversations.
10. Wants to know who's calling/texting/e-mailing you when the phone rings or your cell goes off.

11. A gut feeling in your stomach something doesn't quite feel right (DON'T IGNORE IT! FOLLOW IT!)
12. Doesn't like your friends and suggests you hang out with his friends…ALL the time.
13. Is critical of your family. Suddenly his family surrounds you ALL the time.
14. Hates your work, your boss, your co-workers, tells you he is tired of hearing about them and suggests you find a new 'more suitable job'. *(Suitable? For who? Him???)*
15. Orders for you when you go out to eat, and tells you what to drink, too.
16. Insists on uncomfortable sexual positions, even if you display discomfort carrying them out.
17. **Never, EVER shack-up.** Always marry as this gives you some legal leverage when things fall apart. *(Trust me, they will.)*
18. Insists you move in with him and wants to get rid of your stuff as it reminds him of your exes. (What he is really saying is he wants to get rid of your identity and replace it with what he thinks it should be.)
19. He chooses what you watch on TV and what movies you go to see.

20. Calls you frequently, at work, on your cell, checks your car hood when you get home, reads your odometer on your car.
21. Goes through your laundry checking your underwear and personal effects, looking for signs of you having an affair (*ewwwwww*).
22. Resists your attempts to help him seek help. He doesn't think anything is wrong with him. This is why his actions don't match his words.
23. Checks your call history on your cell phone; hits the redial button on your home phone.
24. Hires a private investigator to tail you or in some cases, does the work himself.
25. Accuses your family of calling too often when in fact their calling patterns are normal.
26. Follows you on twitter and reads posts on your Facebook wall.
27. Accuses you of flirting with the delivery guy, cable man, guy at the store, telemarketer on the phone, etc.
28. Refers to your ex as *expletive, son of a you-know-what, piece of ****, etc.*
29. Calls just before you leave work and times your arrival home *(Fire alarms should be sounding in your head right now. If they're not, you might want to get that checked out...)*

30. Calls during lunchtime to check up on you. Ladies be careful of this one, don't be fooled into thinking he cares about you by doing this.

31. Calls often and plays it off by saying just because he's thinking of you. *(Can you say creepy????)*

32. Loves to read your credit card statements. *(Uh-oh...)*

33. Insists on knowing all your passwords (*Are you kidding me???*)

34. Insists on joint accounts. *(At this point you should have taken off and not wait around for the rest.)* Never combine your finances. Most couples have a joint account from which they pay bills but keep separate savings accounts.

35. Wants you to take out a mortgage/car note, credit card. **DO NOT SIGN FOR ANYTHING! It will ruin your credit!**

36. Did we say not to shack-up? Maybe if I use a nicer term, you will see what I mean. **Do not live in the same house or apartment with this man.** If for some bizarre reason you do, write out and execute a partner agreement, detailing who is responsible for what household expenses, etc.

37. Never buy property with this man. **Never, NEVER.**

38. My personal favorite - never share intimate details of your family members, childhood, stories of your siblings, any sibling rivalry, disputes between family members. Never tell this man anything about your childhood for which you are having issues. He will store it and use it against you in the future.

39. He will wreak havoc with your friends. And that gives him the opportunity to say, you don't need them, I'm all you need, I would never do that to you.

40. He will wreak havoc with your family members, and based on what you told him, he will say, I told you they don't love you, I am the only one who loves you. *(By now you should have left the area, or state or the country).*

41. Did I say he is charming to all women? Even going as far out of his way to engage the server, sales lady, sales person, in useless conversation, and being extremely charming even when it appears to make the person and you uncomfortable.

42. Slams his fist on the table, against the wall, etc. *(Your insides should be quaking by now; think Dr. Jekyll and Mr. Hyde with the severe mood swings.)*

43. Everything eventually revolves around him or he is not happy. He will teach you the difference between selfish and self-centered.
44. He is too nice to your kids at first. Winning them over is the first half of the disarming process. This type of man is known to target single women with children.
45. Is critical of your accomplishments, always seems to redirect the conversation back to him. Also disrespects you and other women, even women in his life (mother, sisters, female cousins, etc.)
46. Talks about himself and his escapades a lot, leaving out his history of abusing women and household pets/small animals. Men who abuse animals tend to abuse women, also.
47. You begin to get the feeling he wants to erase all people and places you have known all your life. *(If you are still there, you need a sharp kick to your posterior to jump-start the leaving. Get out of there now!)*
48. Is uncomfortable with stories about abusive men; finds a way to defend men who commit violence against women. He will even seem to idolize serial killers, excuses their behavior.

49. If he has a copy of <u>Mein Kampf</u> by Adolf Hitler. Defends Adolf's partner suicide with Eva (*What more do you need to hear?*)

50. Wants you to wear what he has chosen for you. Remember that shopping trip that made you giddy with excitement? The one where he pulled out his credit card and bought the whole store for you? And you tweeted and Facebooked about it like there was no tomorrow? Get ready. Remember how he seemed to choose everything, overriding your choices? That is a clue to what is coming your way. You should have left by now.